Scavenger Hike Adventures

Great Smoky Mountains
National Park

*A small sampling of praise from City Slickers,
Pioneer Scouts, and Frontier Explorers*

"Thanks for doing this book and giving a new meaning to hiking!"
— D. N., Indianapolis, Ind.

"Kat and John LaFevre provide detailed clues that help readers discover little-known parts of the Great Smoky Mountains National Park."
— *Southern Living* magazine

". . . one-of-a-kind book designed for all levels of hikers."
— *Mountain Press*

"Big fun for kids and adults." — Great Smoky Mountains Association

". . . an interactive journey where the plants, trees, rocks, and historic relics reveal their secrets and stories to you."
— Joe Guenther, owner of The DayHiker (Outfitter Store)

"Kind of like having a Cherokee Indian, pioneer settler, and mountain explorer hiking along with you."
— Mark Clark, Great Smoky Mountains guide

"Everyone needs a portal between day-to-day life in the modern world and the wondrous world of wilderness. This book is one of the best. By the time the kids find a few hidden treasures, they will be on their way to a lifelong, life-enriching exploration of nature and our national parks."
— Steve Kemp, director of publications for the
Great Smoky Mountains Association and
editor and writer of many classic Smoky Mountains books

"We found things we would have never known were there."
— Camper on Porter's Creek Trail

Help Us Keep This Guide Up to Date

Every effort has been made by the authors and editors to make this guide as accurate and useful as possible. However, many things can change after a guide is published—trails are rerouted, regulations change, facilities come under new management, etc.

We would love to hear from you concerning your experiences with this guide and how you feel it could be improved and kept up to date. While we may not be able to respond to all comments and suggestions, we'll take them to heart and we'll also make certain to share them with the authors. Please send your comments and suggestions to the following address:

The Globe Pequot Press
Reader Response/Editorial Department
P.O. Box 480
Guilford, CT 06437

Or you may e-mail us at:

editorial@GlobePequot.com

Thanks for your input, and happy trails!

Scavenger Hike Adventures
Great Smoky Mountains National Park

Kat and John LaFevre
Illustrated by G Webb

GUILFORD, CONNECTICUT
HELENA, MONTANA
AN IMPRINT OF THE GLOBE PEQUOT PRESS

Falcon and FalconGuides are registered trademarks of Morris Book Publishing, LLC.

Illustrations by G Webb, Gatlinburg, Tennessee
Text design by Lisa Reneson
Map by Lisa Reneson © Morris Book Publishing, LLC
Cover photos: mountains © Mark Karrass/Corbis; Model T © Bill Brooks/Alamy; Elijah Oliver's cabin © Richard Weisser and SmokyPhotos.com; rhododendron © Westend 61/Alamy; authors © M&M Clark

Library of Congress Cataloging-in-Publication Data

LaFevre, Kat.
  Scavenger hike adventures : Great Smoky Mountains National Park / Kat and John LaFevre ; illustrated by G Webb.
    p. cm. — (A falcon guide)
  Includes bibliographical references.
  ISBN: 978-0-7627-4466-4
  1. Hiking—Great Smoky Mountains (N.C. and Tenn.)—Guidebooks. 2. Trails—Great Smoky Mountains National Park (N.C. and Tenn.)—Guidebooks. 3. Treasure hunt (Game)—Great Smoky Mountains National Park (N.C. and Tenn.)—Guidebooks. 4. Great Smoky Mountains National Park (N.C. and Tenn.)—Guidebooks. I. LaFevre, John. II. Title.
  GV199.42.G73L35 2007
  796.510973—dc22   2006035289

Manufactured in the United States of America
First Edition/First Printing

To buy books in quantity for corporate use
or incentives, call **(800) 962–0973**
or e-mail **premiums@GlobePequot.com**.

Scavenger Hike Adventures

Don't *Just* Take a Hike . . . Take a Scavenger Hike Adventure!!!

Contents

1   **"Junglebrook" Noah "Bud" Ogle Farm Trail**   **1**
     0.75-mile loop, about an hour; the trail is rocky,
     shaded; pretty easy

2   **Porter's Creek Trail to Old Hiking Club Cabin**   **15**
     2.0 miles round-trip, 2 to 3 hours; wide trail has long,
     gentle uphill slope; moderate

3   **Laurel Falls Trail to Laurel Falls**   **31**
     stroller accessible and wheelchair do-able; 2.6 miles
     round-trip, about 2 hours; trail is paved, gentle uphill
     slope; popular; pretty easy but not a cakewalk

hike
adventures
marked by X's

Newfound Gap
Road

T E N N E S S

441

Sugarlands
Visitor
Center

X X X
3   9   7

Little River
Road

Carles Cove
X
8

Appalachian Trail

GREAT SMOKY
MOUTAINS
NATIONAL PAR

Lake Fontana

Watch for Waterfalls
on #3, 5, 6 & 8

74

N O R T H

Cosby

X
12

X
11

X   X
6

X   Greenbrier
2

X   X
/14   4

441
X
10

Newfound
Gap Road

Cherokee
Indian
Reservation

441   Old Steam Engine
in Creek on #11

C A R O L I N A

WHAT *IS* A SCAVENGER HIKE ADVENTURE . . . ANYWAY?

The mountains are calling! Grab your family or friend! **A wilderness adventure is waiting for you!**

Scavenger Hike Adventures are challenging and fun for amateur hikers, experienced day hikers, and serious trekkers! Hikes range from an easy half mile to a challenging 10.5 miles and OVER a mile high in elevation!

Six scavenger hikes are kind of **Easy,** four are **Moderate,** and four are **EXTREME!** All 14 hikes lead to exciting discoveries!

Are you up for the challenge? Follow our clues to find . . . a tree clawed open by a bear . . . an ancient Indian footpath . . . a wrecked steam engine that rolled off a mountain over 80 years ago . . . hidden breath-taking mountain . . . a beautiful waterfall view that most visitors never get to see . . . remains of an old Model T . . . pioneer cabins . . . and over 200 other unusual treasures!

Earn 10 points for each treasure that you find and achieve *one of three certificate levels!*
Finally answer the question:
        Are you a ......?
        City Slicker!
        Pioneer Scout!!
        or Frontier Explorer!!!

We have included **Scavenger Hike Adventures** near campgrounds and throughout the national park! **Don't *Just* Take a Hike . . . Take a Scavenger Hike Adventure!**

THE GREAT SMOKY MOUNTAINS NATIONAL PARK

A Treasure beyond Description!

There simply are no words or photographs that can capture the majesty, warmth, and beauty of the mountains or the friendly sound of a little red boomer squirrel chattering in the early morning mist. There is only one way to feel the magic of a waterfall or sense the awe as a deer quietly walks through the forest.

You must experience it!

Please remember that you are entering a very fragile and diverse system of plants, water, and animals that is known and cherished throughout the world. There are over 1,500 unique flowering plants; over 130 different species of trees; and, scientists believe, over 100,000 different life forms.

Please protect our national treasure . . .
The Great Smoky Mountains National Park!

Please . . .

Take Only Pictures

Leave Only Footprints.

WHO ARE YOUR SCAVENGER HIKE ADVENTURE GUIDES?

Kat and John LaFevre are Gatlinburg, Tennessee, locals who live in a log cabin high up in the mountains. They are avid hikers and love the Great Smoky Mountains. They have hiked and researched the trails and visited with many old-timers to discover the hidden natural and historical treasures of the Smokies.

Kat has bachelor's and master's degrees in elementary education. She taught for several years and has worked as a VIP (volunteer in the Great Smoky Mountains National Park). Kat has also assisted with the national park's Outreach Program, an educational community initiative, and is working on her goal to hike all of the 830-plus miles of trails in the national park.

John majored in English and communications and is a business consultant and professional speaker. He has written feature articles for the *Wall Street Journal's National Employment Weekly* and many national magazines. He has also written a business book that was published by Simon & Schuster and issued in three editions. John is a country musician and songwriter when he is not out on the trails or talkin' somewhere.

OUR THANKS

Our thanks to the park rangers, volunteers, and professional employees of the Great Smoky Mountains National Park for the outreach programs, ranger-led hikes, and special park events that were invaluable resources as we researched hidden treasures.

In particular, thanks to George Minnigh, backcountry specialist with the national park system; Ellen Ogle, retired resource education ranger; and Marion Gray, forestry technician. They reviewed our drafts and offered invaluable insight and encouragement. We are fortunate to have them working for all of us in our national park.

Thanks to Annette Hartigan, park librarian; Mike Jenkins, ecologist; Tim Cruze, park ranger; and Don Jones, park volunteer, for assisting us in validating facts and species.

Thanks to Ken Jenkins, nationally acclaimed wildlife photographer, who founded "Wilderness Wildlife Week," an event that brings together wilderness and wildlife experts every year to share stories and knowledge. What a wonderful learning experience.

Thanks to the Great Smoky Mountains Association and Friends of the Smokies, who sponsor many educational programs. These two nonprofit organizations exist for the sole purpose of protecting and enhancing the park for all visitors and future generations.

We also thank esteemed artist and friend, G Webb, for illustrating our book.

A special thanks to Lori LaFevre, Joel Outten, and Mark Bryant for field-testing the trails. Thanks to Amy and Kevin VanDeWater for proofreading, editing, and encouragement. Finally, our thanks again to the Great Smoky Mountains Association for their wonderful library of publications, which were an invaluable resource.

WHAT'S ALL THIS TALK ABOUT BEARS?

Want to see a bear? Keep in mind that most bear sightings occur in the early morning and at dusk. Our favorite way to go "lookin' for bears" is to rent bicycles at the Cades Cove campground area. Try to be the first customers on those mornings when the park does not allow cars into Cades Cove, and bike around the 11-mile loop—just you, your bike, and wildlife! Of course, Cades Cove is also a great place to search for wildlife from your car! Don't miss it!

- There are about 1,500 black bears living in the park. That means there are about two bears for every square mile.

- You'll find bears out and about in the early morning or at dusk, but also throughout the day and night. There could be one around the next bend in the trail. Bears do not want to harm you. They just want to be left alone so they can go about their "bear" business.

- If you see a bear, remain watchful. DO NOT APPROACH IT!!

- NEVER RUN from a black bear!! Slowly back away.

- If a bear is persistent in following you, talk loudly, shout at it, clap your hands, raise your arms to look bigger—throw nonfood objects at it if necessary. (See park visitor centers for additional info.)

- If a black bear attacks you . . . FIGHT BACK!! Never play dead or lie down.

- Bears can run and climb up and down trees much faster than you!

A final note that "bears" consideration: **Don't feed the bears!!** Once a bear tastes peanut butter or fried chicken and potato salad, it wants seconds and thirds. Once bears see people as a food source, they often lose their natural fear of humans and become what are called "nuisance" bears. These bears often must be removed from the park and sometimes *even killed* because they threaten people by getting too close. Remember . . . people food kills bears!

All hikers must assume responsibility for their own actions and safety. All the hikes are on designated portions of Great Smoky Mountains National Park trails. It is impossible to list and describe all potential hazards. National park brochures and publications by the Great Smoky Mountains Association provide additional safety information. The park is a wild area and should be addressed with utmost caution and common sense. Nature may change or alter some of the Scavenger Hike Treasures. The trail search hints will be constantly reviewed and regularly updated. We suggest that you visit our Web site, www.scavengerhikeadventures.com for updates.

Kat   *John*

SCAVENGER HIKE ADVENTURES
TOP-TEN DAY HIKER CHECKLIST

1. Always protect the Great Smoky Mountains National Park! Treat it like the "treasure" it is! Don't pick anything! Don't take anything! Don't leave anything!

2. Stay on the trails! Step lightly! Respect and protect each and every plant and animal in the park!

3. Don't forget to pack your common sense. This is a wilderness area!

4. Water is the most important item for you to bring! Never drink from streams and rivers!

5. Bring snacks or lunch along! Food tastes at least twice as good in the woods!

6. Always plan on some raindrops falling on your head! Bring a poncho! If the weather forecast calls for 100 percent sunshine . . . bring your poncho!

7. Insect repellent is a handy item, especially in the summer!

8. Hiking boots are great! Gym shoes are "fine." Sandals . . . not recommended. Wear flip-flops, and that is just what you will do! When counting steps to find treasures . . . small folks take tall steps and tall folks take small steps!

9. Wet rocks and roots can be very slippery! Please watch your step!

10. Most hikers who have gotten lost . . . had separated from their group and went ahead! Stay with your exploration party, and have a great Scavenger Hike Adventure!

Scavenger Hike Adventure

"Junglebrook"
Noah "Bud" Ogle Farm Trail

WHY THIS IS A GREAT TRAIL! This Scavenger Hike Adventure is awesome! You will find a pioneer cabin and barn that are about 120 years old and a working water-powered grinding mill deep in the forest! The pioneers called this area "Junglebrook" because the woods are overgrown like a jungle! You'll cross many log footbridges over small streams. You'll even cross some streams with no bridges! You'll search for an old-fashioned water pipe, umbrellas over your head, a "drive-thru" pioneer barn, a hidden hillside spring, a place where a bear might be napping, and much more!

WHERE'S THE TRAIL? From the Sugarlands Visitor Center, go north on U.S. Highway 441 into Gatlinburg. Turn right (east) at **Stoplight #8,** Historic Nature Trail/Airport Road. (Stoplights in

Gatlinburg are all numbered with big signs.) Follow the signs to Roaring Fork Motor Nature Trail and the Ogle Place. Parking is on the right.

ABOUT THE TRAIL: This Scavenger Hike Adventure is on a beautiful, EASY trail that crosses streams and runs along LeConte Creek. There are rocks along the trail ranging in size from beach balls to beanbag chairs and much larger! It is pretty much all level, with a couple of small hills to climb. "Junglebrook" is mostly shaded in the thick woods, making this a VERY COOL trail! If this trail wasn't free, we would GUARANTEE double your money back if you don't think this Scavenger Hike Adventure is awesome!

HOW LONG IS THIS HIKE? This Scavenger Hike Adventure is a 0.75-mile loop and will take about an hour to complete.

THINGS TO HUNT FOR

(Earn 10 points for each treasure you find.)

1

FIND THE QUARTZ ROCK!
Smack-Dab between Two Trees!
(Near start of trail before Marker #1)

SPECIAL HINT: You'll find this reddish-brown and white quartz rock smack-dab between two trees! After you find it, look around! Most of the trees that you see here today were not here when this was a pioneer farm. In fact, all around you were open fields and a big apple orchard! As you head up to the cabin, you'll be walking on the old road that led to Gatlinburg (back then, Gatlinburg was called White Oak Flats). Farmers needed their land for food, so the roads often ran beside or at times even *in* the creek so land would not be wasted. The Ogle family planted and raised all their own food!

10 POINTS

2

FIND GRANNY'S WINDOW!

(In the old log cabin)

SPECIAL HINT: Find the small window with a wooden "door." It was called **"granny's window"**! Granny Ogle could sit by the window and open it for fresh air or to shoot at foxes that were after her chickens (according to a former resident). Women had to protect the family's food from wild animals, especially when the men were away. Can you believe there were four beds in this one room! This early pioneer cabin is about 120 years old!

10 POINTS

3

FIND THE LOFT

Where the Boys Would Sleep! (Look up!)

SPECIAL HINT: Look up and find where the Ogle boys would sleep! Sorry! No girls were allowed to sleep up there in the loft! Bud and Cindy Ogle and their four boys and four girls lived in this cabin! At first the cabin only had one room, but they needed more space for all the young'uns, so they built another room on the other side of the fireplace! Check it out! Cindy called the original room of the cabin "the house," and the room they added on she called "t'uther"! **10 POINTS**

4

FIND THE RHODODENDRON JUNGLE!
(Head into the woods past Marker #3—
step on the rocks to cross the stream.)

SPECIAL HINT: Look all around you! Rhododendrons have long, narrow, leathery evergreen leaves. They are so thick here that the pioneers called this area "Junglebrook"! Imagine in the summer when the rhododendron flowers were all in bloom! Mountains! Green forest! Flowering bushes! White rushing waters! "Junglebrook" was a beautiful and peaceful place! It still is! **10 POINTS**

5

FIND THE HUGE STUMPS of Old Chestnut Trees!
(Go 40 steps past the log footbridge.)

SPECIAL HINT: Start lookin'! All the huge chestnut trees died over 70 years ago from a bad blight (disease). It was said that cabins made from chestnut trees would last forever because the wood would never rot. The chestnuts were delicious, and bears

were much bigger back then because they ate lots and lots of
chestnuts! Hogs loved them, squirrels loved them,
wild turkeys loved them, and people loved them
too! Ahhh . . . chestnuts roasting o'er an open fire!   **10 POINTS**

6
FIND A TREE That Looks like Twins!
(On the right side of the trail—between Markers #5 and #6)

SPECIAL HINT: Find the two trunks of a tree that are joined
together at the bottom. From this tree, walk **42** steps toward
Marker #6 and search for another twin tree on the right! I guess
you could say you found "twin twin twees"! The twunks of
these twees, er, the trunks of these trees were split by nature
when they were very young. The trees may have
been struck by lightning or chewed on by an animal to make them split and grow twin trunks!   **10 POINTS**

7
FIND AN OLD ROCK WALL Built by the Pioneers!
(On both sides of the trail)

SPECIAL HINT: The Smoky Mountains is a very rocky place.
Rock walls were built by pioneers to clear the rocks off the
land so crops could be planted, cabins could be built, and
cows could be kept out of the garden and in the pasture. The
pioneer children helped build these walls! The
area all around you was once a large cow pas-
ture. After you find the wall, *moooove* along!   **10 POINTS**

8

FIND WHERE THE HONEYMOON CABIN Once Stood!

(About 30 steps past the rock wall—on the left of the trail)

SPECIAL HINT: A huge stack of rocks marks the spot of the "honeymoon" or "weaner" cabin. Bud and Cindy Ogle would let their sons and their new brides live here for one year until they could build a cabin of their own. When the Ogle girls married, they moved on with their husbands.

10 POINTS

9

FIND AN OLD-FASHIONED WATER PIPE!

(Search across the trail from the honeymoon cabin.)

SPECIAL HINT: Find a long log that was carved out to carry water. ***Please stay on the trail.*** You'll see such **log flumes** in use in about five minutes. The Ogles didn't have metal pipes, but these carved-out logs worked just great to bring water from LeConte Creek to the mill!

10 POINTS

PROTECT THE GREAT SMOKY MOUNTAINS NATIONAL PARK

10

FIND "UMBRELLAS" over Your Head!

(After you pass the carved-out hollow log—
take 12 steps and turn right onto the side path.)

SPECIAL HINT: Follow the side path all the way down to LeConte Creek! Small children should be escorted down to the stream. ***Remember . . . rocks may be slippery!*** When you get to the stream, look straight up to find the "umbrellas" over your head! These leaves are from the umbrella magnolia tree. The Smoky Mountains get more rain than almost anywhere else in our whole country. In fact, about 7 feet of rain or more falls in the upper elevations every year. Umbrellas sure come in handy in the Smokies! These "umbrellas" are not available in the winter or early spring, when the leaves are gone.

10 POINTS

11

FIND THE OLD PIONEER FAMILY TUB MILL!

(On the right of the trail)

SPECIAL HINT: Walk inside, go up the wooden steps, and then peek down through the hole and see the waterwheel that turns the corn-grinding machine. This **tub mill** would grind corn into cornmeal, and then the Ogles could make corn bread! There used to be about 13 tub mills on this creek! That's why back then they called this stream "Mill Creek." The mill was a popular place for the mountain folks to get together and "spin yarns," tell tall tales, and catch up on news of the locals while the young'uns played in the creek. People were always "milling around" the mill!

10 POINTS

12

STOP AND PLOP DOWN on a Rock!

(Just past the tub mill)

SPECIAL HINT: Sit on a rock and listen to the water to get these points! See the water . . . hear the water . . . and then follow the hollowed-out logs upstream to the log dam and see where they catch the water! *Be careful on the slippery rocks!*

10 POINTS

13

FIND WHERE A BEAR Might Be Taking a Nap!

(Head way up the hill—to the *very top*—
look on the left of the nature trail sign.)

SPECIAL HINT: Look for a big flat rock that is ALMOST, but not quite, level with the ground, like a platform that completely fills the area between the two trees. Stand on the rock, look away from the path, and find the **dark holes in the rocks** on the side of the hill. Do you think a bear could be taking a nap in there? Remember! Now that "Junglebrook" is part of our national park, many of the "locals" that live here today make their homes among the rocks and in the trees!

10 POINTS

14

FIND TARZAN'S GRAPEVINE!

(Walk up the trail and then take 20 steps back from Marker #9
toward Marker #8—look to the left.)

SPECIAL HINT: Look deep into the woods on the left and find
a humongous woody wild grapevine high up in
the trees! You might just be tempted to give a
Tarzan yell! On second thought . . . let's not dis-
turb the "locals"!

10 POINTS

15

FIND THE BOULDER That Is Bigger
than Your Car or Truck!

(On the right of the trail)

SPECIAL HINT: You don't need a special hint for this one!
You'll know when you find THIS giant boulder! Can you find
the thin strand of **white quartz rock** that
runs through this boulder? Veer to the
right after you pass
the boulder, and
stay on the
rocky trail.

10 POINTS

16

FIND THE TREE That a Giant Woodpecker Punched Holes in Big Enough to Stick Your Hand inside the Tree!

(25 steps up the trail from the corner of the big boulder you just found—look on the left.)

SPECIAL HINT: A pileated woodpecker is a giant black and red-crested bird that pecks giant oval holes in trees. It is one of the largest and loudest woodpeckers in all of North America! It looks like the famous cartoon character, Woody Woodpecker. If Porky Pig was standing at your side he would probably look up and say, *"That's all, folks."* By the way, there are hundreds of wild hogs in the national park, but none of them speak English.

10 POINTS

17

FIND A PERSON IN YOUR GROUP Who Has Some Food or a Snack!

(Explore around backpacks or bulging pockets.)

SPECIAL HINT: Say, *"Doh-YUST zah-ah-geest?"* That is Cherokee for "What have you got to eat?" Cherokee Indians lived all around these mountains long before the white settlers came. Cherokees still live in these mountains on the Qualla Indian Reservation in Cherokee, North Carolina. **Chief Sequoya**

saw white settlers holding paper with writing on it, and he called it "talking leaves." He wanted Cherokees to have "talking leaves," so he made a symbol for every Cherokee sound and Cherokees began to learn their new written language! So . . . keep reading this "talking leaf" and head on down the trail!

10 POINTS

18
FIND THE WOODPECKER CAFE!
(Near Marker #10)

SPECIAL HINT: This tree is full of holes made by a woodpecker. There may be no blinking neon light, but this is definitely a "Woodpecker Cafe." There must be some delicious bugs being served here!

10 POINTS

19
FIND A WALL OF ROOTS!
(Hike for about 5 minutes—cross streams several times—look on the left of the trail.)

SPECIAL HINT: Look for two trees that fell over and created an incredible **wall of roots.** Nature is amazing!

10 POINTS

20

FIND A "DRIVE-THRU" BARN!

(Near Marker #12)

SPECIAL HINT: Walk through—the drive-thru! This **drive-thru barn** is over 120 years old! Can you believe Bud Ogle built this barn almost all by himself? Bud and his sons could load hay on a wagon and then drive right through the barn to unload the hay and feed the animals! There were a few other buildings on this old farmstead, including a smokehouse, a springhouse, a hog pen, and a corncrib. Travelers on the wagon road in front of the barn would stop by to feed and water their animals. They were charged a "toll" (small fee) by the Ogles for this service.

10 POINTS

21

FIND THE HIDDEN MOUNTAIN SPRING!

(Past the barn—on the side of the hill)

SPECIAL HINT: This hole is where the Ogle family got their water from a spring. Remember the hollowed-out logs you saw at the tub mill? The Ogles used the same kind of logs to bring water from this spring all the way to the back porch of their cabin, where all the washin' was done. Most folks had to carry their water in big heavy buckets, and that was hard work! The Ogles were one of the first families in the area to have automatic "running water"! Their neighbors thought this was pretty cool!

10 POINTS

CONGRATULATIONS!

You have just completed a

Great Smoky Mountains National Park

Scavenger Hike Adventure!

"Junglebrook"
Noah "Bud" Ogle Farm Trail

10 points for each item found

Total Score _____

Certified Achievement Level _____

50 to 100 points: *City Slicker*

Over **100 to 180** points: *Pioneer Scout*

Over **180** points: *Frontier Explorer*

Name(s): _____

_____

Witness(es) thereof: _____

Date: _____

Journal Notes

The people on this hike were:

_____

_____

_____

The weather was:

_____

_____

_____

We saw:

_____

_____

_____

More about our adventure:

_____

_____

_____

_____

Scavenger Hike Adventure

Porter's Creek Trail to

Old Hiking Club Cabin

WHY THIS IS A GREAT TRAIL! This Scavenger Hike Adventure winds along the beautiful Porter's Creek rapids in the quieter and less busy Greenbrier section of the national park. This trail is loaded with historic artifacts from the old pioneer days! Find the special **mountain rock** where the pioneers "courted" (went on dates) and the remains of a Model T hidden deep in the forest! You will search for a special tree that the Indians used, cross log footbridges, and stand inside an old "refrigerator" (springhouse) that is still cooled by running water! You will find an old cabin with bunk beds built right into the walls, an old outhouse, and much more! We'll give you some good hints, but you can't be dozin' on this hike. Pick yourself up by the bootstraps! Let's go!

WHERE'S THE TRAIL? From the Sugarlands Visitor Center go north on U.S. Highway 441 into Gatlinburg. Veer right at

Stoplight #3, just past the Hard Rock Cafe. (Stoplights in Gatlinburg are all numbered with big signs.) Follow U.S. Highway 321 approximately 6 miles to the Greenbrier entrance of Great Smoky Mountains National Park. Turn right. Travel the narrow road along the incredibly beautiful white water of the Little Pigeon River, and follow the signs to Porter's Creek trailhead. You'll pass the ranger station and go deep into the woods past the picnic area. There's a parking area at the trailhead. You will never regret the beautiful drive to get to this Scavenger Hike Adventure! There will be *at least* five "Ooohs" and "Ahhhs" along the way!

ABOUT THE TRAIL: This Scavenger Hike Adventure is a gentle **uphill hike** on a trail wide enough for an automobile. That means you can look forward to a gentle **downhill slope** all the way back. This hike is not very hard—a MODERATE hike.

HOW LONG IS THIS HIKE? This Scavenger Hike Adventure is 2.0 miles round-trip and will take 2 to 3 hours to complete.

THINGS TO HUNT FOR

(Earn 10 points for each treasure you find.)

1

FIND THE OLD CORNFIELD
That No Longer Looks like a Cornfield!
(Cross the vehicle gate to start the trail—
look to the right of the trail.)

SPECIAL HINT: Search for a group of more than 50 trees with grayish bark that are straight, very tall, thin, and look like giant pencils! These are yellow poplar trees (tulip trees), which often grow up in what was **once a cornfield.** Some folks think the leaves or the spring blossoms on this tree are shaped like tulips. To get the points, "erase" those pencil-shaped trees from your mind and visualize the cornfield!

Greenbrier was once a bustling farming community with more than 800 people living here! Isn't that amazing?

10 POINTS

2

FIND THE TWIN YELLOW BIRCH TREE
That the Indians Used!

(As you hike up the gentle slope, look to the right
—it is only 2 feet off the trail.)

SPECIAL HINT: This yellow birch tree has split into two trunks, and you might think it looks like a "twin" tree. It has yellowish/silverish (sometimes shiny) bark that in places looks like shredded paper! The grooves/lines in the bark run horizontal to the ground instead of vertical. That is a major clue! What is cool about this unusual tree is that there is oil in the bark—pioneers and Indians could use it to start fires *even when the bark was wet!* We get lots of rain in the Smoky Mountains, so this tree was probably very much appreciated!

10 POINTS

3

FIND THE "DEVIL'S WALKING STICK"!

(On the right side of the trail—only 2 feet off the trail)

SPECIAL HINT: As you walk up the hill, first find the **cliff on the left in an open area** overlooking the creek—way down there! On the opposite side of the trail from this cliff area, find a tree about the thickness of a hiking stick. It is covered with hundreds of thorns! Pioneers called it the "Devil's Walking Stick." It looks like a hiking stick with thorns! Ouch!

10 POINTS

4

FIND THE "MOUNTAIN ROCK"
Where Young Pioneers Went on Dates!
(On the left side of the trail)

SPECIAL HINT: This giant rock *does* have a shape like a mountain, and your eyes would have to be closed to miss this natural wonder! Young pioneers would meet here to "court" (to go on a date). Obviously, this was a long time before funnel cakes, miniature golf, and the sky lift in Gatlinburg were invented!

10 POINTS

5

FIND THE GIANT TURTLE ROCK!
(About 175 steps past the mountain rock, stop and look ahead about 30 yards on the right side of the trail—find the "turtle" sticking its head out of a shell.)

SPECIAL HINT: This may sound like *Ripley's Believe It or Not,* but the pioneer young'uns who got bored dating at the "mountain rock" would also date at the "turtle rock"! It really *does* look like a turtle sticking its head out of its shell!

10 POINTS

6

FIND A SALAMANDER!

(Stop at the little mountain stream that crosses the path.)

SPECIAL HINT: Carefully lift up stones or small branches that are in or along the water. Underneath these rocks and sticks are the homes of salamanders. In the Smokies, salamanders grow from ½-inch to over 2 feet long! *Be gentle; don't ever put a rock back on top of a salamander or keep it out of water for more than a minute because its skin will dry out.* There are more salamanders in this national park than the total of birds, deer, bears, and all other mammals combined!

10 POINTS

7

FIND THE GIANT OLD OAK TREE
That Is Searching for Water!

(Next to the mountain stream on the right side of the trail)

SPECIAL HINT: The roots are growing all around rocks to search for water! In the Smokies you'll see lots of tree roots growing on top of the ground because they have trouble getting through the rocks. The Smoky Mountains is a very rocky place!

There are many very old trees in the park. The Great Smoky Mountains National Park also has more **champion trees** (largest of the species) than any other national park in the United States!

10 POINTS

8

FIND AND SIT ON THE LOG BENCH!
(On the left)

SPECIAL HINT: This hike is a gradual uphill climb, and this is a mandatory break point. You deserve the break and the points for making it this far!

10 POINTS

9

FIND AN AWESOME CASCADE!
(35 steps past the bench)

SPECIAL HINT: A cascade happens when water flows over and around rocks. If the water level here is normal, you will see a breathtaking cascade in the creek at this point. It is a great spot to have a snack—and definitely a place to pause and relax for a minute!

10 POINTS

10

FIND A DYNAMITE HOLE
That Was Drilled in a Rock!

(A couple of feet to the right of the center of the trail)

SPECIAL HINT: Look down! Keep searching as you walk up the trail! In the 1930s, during the Great Depression, President Franklin D. Roosevelt started the Civilian Conservation Corps (CCC). More than 4,000 unemployed young men from all over the United States were hired to help build many of the trails, roads, and stone bridges in this park and were paid $30 per month and were required by CCC rules to send most of the money back home. These young men lived in camps throughout the park and sometimes used dynamite to blast rocks out of the way.

10 POINTS

11

FIND THE NEARLY HALF-MILE-LONG ROCK WALL!

(Look deep into the woods on the right.)

SPECIAL HINT: Keep looking to the right, up on the ridge, to find the wall. Pioneers had to clear the rocks off their land so they could plant crops and build cabins. "VanderBill" Whaley was a wealthy settler who got his nickname from the wealthy Vanderbilt family. (He was not related to them.) He lived here in Greenbrier with his wife and 10 children. His daughters did a lot of the rock work around their house. Rock walls also helped keep animals out of garden areas and often followed along property lines.

10 POINTS

12

FIND THE 13 ROCK STEPS That Lead up to "VanderBill's" Homesite!

(On the right side of the trail)

SPECIAL HINT: *Be careful* as you walk up the rock steps to pay a visit to this old pioneer's homesite! *It is always wise to look before you step, just to be sure you do not step on a Smoky Mountain critter (possibly a snake). Also watch where you reach with your hands, just to be on the safe side!* VanderBill's daughters were very proud of the wall and the steps they helped build leading to their cabin. How did the girls move all of those heavy rocks, anyway? The rocks were put on sleds and then pulled to the wall!

10 POINTS

13

FIND "VANDERBILL'S" FIREPLACE!

(Follow the path through the bushes at the top of the rock steps.)

SPECIAL HINT: Find the fireplace, and imagine where this big four-room home was located. Remember VanderBill was wealthy! He also owned a mill! If you had your own mill, you could grind your *own* corn and also charge others a

"toll" to grind *their* corn. Having a mill could provide extra income for a family.

10 POINTS

14

FIND THE CELLAR
Where the Whaleys Kept Potatoes!

("Warm" your back at the fireplace, where the fire would
have been—then look out and down at the ground.)

SPECIAL HINT: Look for a low spot or depression in the
ground. This area was the cellar. It was a *cool* place to store
things that needed to *stay cool*. How COOL is
that? Carefully head back down the 13 steps to
the trail.

10 POINTS

15

FIND A "HEADACHE CURE" at the Bridge!

(Look to the right as you stand on the bridge.)

SPECIAL HINT: Find an evergreen plant. Think . . . very long
leaves and very long name—**rhododendron!** You'll find rhododendrons throughout the Smokies. They bloom in the late
spring and summer. These shrubs in front of you are **rosebay**
rhododendrons and have beautiful white or light pink blooms.
Catawba rhododendrons grow in the upper elevations and
have beautiful big purple and pink blooms! Pioneers made tool

handles out of the wood. Cherokee Indians carved pipes and toys out of this shrub and believed a leaf on the forehead would cure a headache! Please use your own headache cure! ***Don't ever pick or harm any plant in the park. All plants are protected by our national park laws.***

◯

10 POINTS

16

FIND THE REMAINS OF AN ANTIQUE MODEL T!

(Find the steps leading to a cemetery on the right side of the trail. From these steps continue on the trail for 115 steps—look to the right, and peer into the woods about 30 yards or so.)

SPECIAL HINT: Look for rusted fenders and parts! Notice how wide the trail is? Why do you think it is so wide? Hint: Don't you wish you had a Model T right now? By the way, those steps that you passed lead to a cemetery with headstones marked WHALEY, OWNBY, and PROFFITT. They were some of the earliest settlers, and their names are *still* popular throughout the county.

◯

10 POINTS

Now, just enjoy the hike! When you come to the split, or Y, in the trail, bear to the right. When you come to a small sign that says HISTORIC FARM SITE, *head 200 yards to the right.*

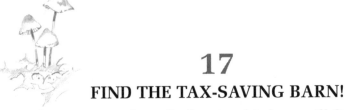

17

FIND THE TAX-SAVING BARN!

(Don't worry about finding it—this barn will find you!)

SPECIAL HINT: The second level of the barn extends farther out than the lower level. It is called a **cantilever barn** and is a copy of a German design. In Germany you only had to pay taxes for the amount of actual ground your barn was sitting on. You didn't have to pay taxes for the larger overhanging part of the second level. Pioneer John Messer built this barn in 1875, more than 130 years ago!

10 POINTS

18

FIND AND THEN STAND INSIDE AN OLD "REFRIGERATOR"!

(Go straight through the barn—follow the short path to the springhouse.)

SPECIAL HINT: Water from the spring would flow right through

the springhouse and keep potatoes, eggs, milk, and other foods cooled. Go ahead, stand inside the "pioneer refrigerator"!

10 POINTS

19

FIND THE BOXWOOD BUSHES!

(On the right as you face the front of the cabin)

SPECIAL HINT: These bushes are not native to the park. They were planted to decorate around the cabin.
There are small dark-green leaves on the round-shaped boxwoods.

10 POINTS

20

FIND THREE ROUND MILLSTONES!

(In the area in front of the cabin)

SPECIAL HINT: They look like bicycle-size round wheels, except they are made out of stone. They are half buried in the yard. The round stones would spin around and against one another in a tub mill and crunch down the corn into cornmeal. Don't you wish you had some corn bread and beans right now?

10 POINTS

21
FIND THE BUNK BEDS!
(Attached to the walls of the cabin)

SPECIAL HINT: Go inside and explore throughout this cabin! Years ago the cabin was used by a hiking club. Check out the amazing inside lock on the back door of the cabin. It looks like it was designed to keep out big black bears! Can you figure out how the lock works? If you can, it's worth five bonus points!

10 POINTS

22
FIND THE OUTHOUSE!
(Out back of the cabin)

SPECIAL HINT: Follow the path out back, out yonder! You do not have to go inside or even get close to the outhouse to get the points!

10 POINTS

CONGRATULATIONS!

You have just completed a

Great Smoky Mountains National Park

Scavenger Hike Adventure!

Porter's Creek Trail to Old Hiking Club Cabin

10 points for each item found

Total Score _____

Certified Achievement Level _____

50 to 100 points: *City Slicker*

Over **100 to 180** points: *Pioneer Scout*

Over **180** points: *Frontier Explorer*

Name(s): _____

_____

Witness(es) thereof: _____

Date: _____

Journal Notes

The people on this hike were:

_____

_____

_____

_____

The weather was:

_____

_____

_____

_____

We saw:

_____

_____

_____

_____

_____

More about our adventure:

_____

_____

_____

_____

_____

Scavenger Hike Adventure

Laurel Falls Trail to Laurel Falls

WHY THIS IS A GREAT TRAIL! This Scavenger Hike Adventure is on a beautiful mountain trail that you DON'T WANT TO MISS! It leads to Laurel Falls, which has an incredible 85-foot drop along a beautiful rock face! What a great spot to relax and have some trail mix! You will find an awesome view of this double waterfall that most visitors will never get to see! You will search for a stream that *never* runs dry, a favorite snack of Smoky Mountain northern flying squirrels, jammed up rocks, and mountain views that are simply breathtaking! You will find some great "Kodak" or "digital" moments on this trail!

WHERE'S THE TRAIL? From the Sugarlands Visitor Center (an awesome "must-see" place to visit!) the trail is 3.8 miles southwest on Little River Road. There is no sign for Little River Road, so just follow the signs toward Cades Cove, Townsend, and Elkmont. If you enter the parking lot at Sugarlands Visitor Center, turn right as you leave the parking lot to get on Little River Road. The falls and the parking area for the trail are well marked.

ABOUT THE TRAIL: This pretty EASY trail was so popular that it was paved in the 1960s to prevent erosion and is now **accessible for strollers and do-able for wheelchairs.** You will find benches and rocks along the way to take a break or two! It is a gradual ascent of only 300 feet in a mile, but the benches still come in handy for most folks! Rocks are slippery around the falls. *Be careful!* There are some sheer drops as you get closer to the falls. *Watch the kids!* Actually, there is an upper and a lower falls! Two waterfalls for only one hike! Gotta be one of the best deals around town—even beats those free samples of fudge!

HOW LONG IS THIS HIKE? This Scavenger Hike Adventure is about 1.3 miles to the falls (2.6 miles round-trip) and will take most pioneers less than 2 hours.

THINGS TO HUNT FOR

(Earn 10 points for each treasure you find.)

1

FIND MOUNTAIN LAUREL AND RHODODENDRON!

(Near Marker #1)

SPECIAL HINT: Look all around! You are standing right in front of rhododendron and mountain laurel bushes, two of the most popular shrubs in the entire park! To get the points, figure out which is which! Here's how to tell the difference between the two: Long leaves equal long name **(rhododendron),** and shorter leaves equal shorter name **(laurel).** They both have dark-green, thick, leathery leaves. Their flowers bloom all along this trail in the spring (mountain laurel) and summer (rhododendron), and the leaves stay green year-round! Pioneers actually called rhododendron "laurel" and called mountain laurel "ivy." Now you know why this is called *Laurel* Falls Trail!

10 POINTS

2
FIND THE JUNGLE!
(45 steps from Marker #1)

SPECIAL HINT: "No lions, no tigers, just bears, oh my!" The rhododendron grows so thick here that it feels like a jungle! The rhododendron was so hard to walk through that pioneers called it a "laurel hell." Peer into the woods and find the tangled shrubs. The rhododendron leaves are also "thermometers"! When the leaves darken and droop, it is about 32 degrees! At around 20 degrees the leaves roll up, and at 0 degrees the leaves roll up as tight as a pencil! How cool is that? A free outdoor thermometer!

10 POINTS

3
FIND A PINE TREE That Was Killed by Southern Pine Beetles!
(12 steps past Marker #2 on the left)

SPECIAL HINT: This pine tree was killed by an insect known as the southern pine beetle. Woodpeckers probably went after the beetle larvae and pecked little holes in the tree to find them. Dead trees become "home" for many forest critters, including salamanders, small mammals, and insects!

10 POINTS

4
FIND THE SECOND-GROWTH FOREST!
(At Marker #3 look down in the "holler.")

SPECIAL HINT: Find lots of smaller trees! This area was logged and also had a huge forest fire. That is why the trees in the "holler" are smaller than a lot of the older trees that live farther up the trail past the waterfall. The loggers didn't go that high up the mountain to cut down trees. In fact, ¾ of a mile past Laurel Falls are some of the oldest trees in the park! You can find trees up there that are hundreds of years old!

10 POINTS

5
FIND THE TREES Twisted by the Wind!
(50 steps from Marker #3—on the right—look up.)

SPECIAL HINT: The high winds can cause branches to curve and grow in strange directions! We mean *really* strange directions!

10 POINTS

6
FIND A TREE Growing Right through an 8-Foot-High Boulder!
(Between Markers #3 and #4)

SPECIAL HINT: You really don't need a hint on this one. Just look to the right and find the tree that broke through a boulder as it grew. This tree was so determined to grow through this rock we should probably name it "Rocky"!

10 POINTS

7

FIND THE BENCH BY THE STREAM
That Never Runs Dry!
(Just past Marker #5)

SPECIAL HINT: Take a break! Of the more than 2,000 miles of streams in the Great Smoky Mountains, this one never runs dry! Deer, bears, snakes, otters, coyotes, and salamanders are a few of the animals that drink from this stream. Many plants and trees thrive along the mountain streams. ***Never drink from a mountain stream*** unless you first treat the water with chemicals or boil it! Microscopic critters live in the water and can make you very sick! Hey! Find the "octopus" behind the bench!

10 POINTS

8

FIND ROOTS CLIMBING ON AND OVER
a Large Group of Rocks!
(After a sharp left turn at a group of jagged rocks, hike up the hill—look on the right.)

SPECIAL HINT: Due to erosion, there's not much soil up here, but there are lots of rocks in the Smokies! The trees have to send out roots searching for soil and water. Can you match up a root with its tree? The roots go over, under, around, and through

rocks to get something to eat and drink! As one
tree said to another, "Where is a Food City when
you need it?"

10 POINTS

9

FIND THE SMOKY MOUNTAIN
"Produce Department"!

(Across the trail from Marker #6—
look to the left in the woods for blueberry bushes.)

SPECIAL HINT: Squirrels, chipmunks, birds,
and, of course, bears love this area because
of all the produce—nuts (acorns),
berries, and seeds. To a bear, this area
is "blueberry heaven" or
maybe even "bearadise"!
Sit on the log bench to see a
blueberry patch.

10 POINTS

10

FIND BLANKET MOUNTAIN!

(At Marker #7 look for the highest mountain
peak in the distance.)

SPECIAL HINT: In 1802 surveyors were establishing the bound-
ary line for a treaty with the Cherokee Indians. A brightly col-
ored blanket was hung on a tree on top of this mountain to help
mark the spot. Ever since then, that highest peak has been
called Blanket Mountain. This is definitely a "Kodak" or "digi-

tal" moment! If you feel the urge you might want to say, **"Ooosh sgwah nickt!"** Cherokee for, "That's incredible!" Cherokee Indians lived around the Smoky Mountains long before white settlers arrived. They called the Smoky Mountains "Shaconage" (pronounced *shuh-KON-a-gee*), which means "land of blue smoke."

◯

10 POINTS

11

FIND THE GROUP OF JAMMED UP ROCKS!

(About 46 steps past Marker #8—look on the right)

SPECIAL HINT: These rocks were pushed up from pressure deep inside the earth. They were kind of "squished" out of the earth. Some scientists believe the continents slowly collided millions of years ago, causing this tremendous pressure. It is believed the Smoky Mountains are more than 260 million years old and many of the rocks here are more than 600 million years old! Whoa!

◯

10 POINTS

12

FIND THE ROCK TRIPE!

(Near Marker #9)

SPECIAL HINT: Look up high on the boulders to your right. This **rock tripe** looks like brownish (sometimes greenish) crumpled leaves. It is a scaly **lichen** (pronounced *LIKE-in*), a combination of algae and fungus, and it grows right on the rock. The rock tripe has acid in it that gradually eats away at the rock. The very tiny particles of broken rock eventually become soil. Rock tripe is a favorite snack of **northern flying squirrels!** Look! Up in the sky! Is it a bird? Is it a plane? No, it's a northern flying squirrel! Actually they are nocturnal, so you'll usually only see them at night, and they generally fly around in higher elevations.

10 POINTS

13
FIND THE DYNAMITE HOLE!
(Go 5 steps past Marker #9—search on the right.)

SPECIAL HINT: Workers had to dynamite and blast through the mountain when they built this trail years ago. Look around for a round hole drilled in the rock to hold a stick of dynamite!

10 POINTS

14
FIND BRIGHT YELLOW LICHEN!

(Past Marker #9 on the right side of the trail—on the rocks)

SPECIAL HINT: This lichen looks like bright yellow spray paint on the rocks. Lichen comes in many different colors. Scientists estimate that there are more than 600 kinds of lichen in this national park! This is a bright one!

10 POINTS

15
FIND THE DRIPPING ROCKS!

(On the right)

SPECIAL HINT: You'll know you have found them when you see a big rock you can sit on right in front of the dripping rocks.

10 POINTS

16

FIND GALAX—The Shiny Leaf Used by Florists!

(Above the dripping rocks)

SPECIAL HINT: Look for the green shiny leaves growing right above the dripping rock ledge. The leaves are shaped kind of like fat hearts, and the plants are quite short and low to the ground. The leaves turn crimson in the fall. Mountain folks earned money gathering the galax (*say GAY-lax*) leaves for florists. ***Remember: Never pick anything . . . these plants are protected by national park laws. Those who break the laws could be given a very sizable fine.***

10 POINTS

17

FIND LAUREL FALLS!

(Follow your ears.)

SPECIAL HINT: Laurel Branch tumbles down from Cove Mountain about 46 feet before it lands in the pool! Then the pool spills over a ledge and drops another 39 feet! Whoa! It rains a lot in the Smoky Mountains (more than 7 feet each year in the higher elevations), which helps make the beautiful waterfalls!

10 POINTS

18

FIND THE VIEW of the Upper and Lower Falls!

(50 steps past the bench at the falls)

SPECIAL HINT: *Walk very carefully* up the unpaved rocky, rooty trail past the falls for another 50 steps. Turn around and you will see the entire upper and lower parts of the falls! Most visitors never see this view. Awesome!

10 POINTS

CONGRATULATIONS!

You have just completed a

Great Smoky Mountains National Park

Scavenger Hike Adventure!

Laurel Falls Trail
to Laurel Falls

10 points for each item found

Total Score _____

Certified Achievement Level _____

50 to 100 points:

City Slicker

Over **100 to 160** points:

Pioneer Scout

Over **160** points:

Frontier Explorer

Name(s): _____

_____

Witness(es) thereof: _____

Date: _____

Journal Notes

The people on this hike were: _____

_____

_____

_____

The weather was: _____

_____

_____

_____

We saw: _____

_____

_____

_____

_____

More about our adventure: _____

_____

_____

_____

_____

_____

Scavenger Hike Adventure

Appalachian Trail
to Charlie's Bunion

WHY THIS IS A GREAT TRAIL! This Extreme Scavenger Hike Adventure takes place on the world famous Appalachian Trail! This is the "Real McCoy," the "Big Kahuna," **one of the longest continuous trails on planet Earth** (2,175 miles long from Georgia to Maine)! The AT runs along a ridge, and you will find breathtaking views of North Carolina mountains on one side and postcard views of Tennessee mountains on the other! You will find Mount LeConte's landslide, Icewater Spring backcountry campsite, a breathtaking 1,000-foot sheer cliff drop, and a view of the highest point in all the Smokies *from* some of the highest points! People from all around the world have hiked the AT! ***Now it's your turn!***

WHERE'S THE TRAIL? From the Sugarlands Visitor Center, travel on U.S. Highway 441 toward Cherokee, North Carolina, to Newfound Gap (13 winding mountain miles with incredible scenic pullouts all along the way). Park at Newfound Gap; you'll see the trailhead sign for the AT as you head up the ridge.

ABOUT THE TRAIL: This part of the AT is very rocky, sometimes steep and narrow, sometimes muddy, and runs along a high-elevation ridge leading to Charlie's Bunion, a bare rock pinnacle overlooking many majestic valleys below. This is an EXTREME hike! We recommend that you start the hike midmorning to allow time for the clouds to clear off the trail! *Caution: There are exposed cliffs as you get closer to the peak!*

HOW LONG IS THIS HIKE? This hike is 8.0 miles round-trip and will take about 5 hours. We suggest you take a lunch and a nap at Charlie's Bunion!

THINGS TO HUNT FOR
(Earn 10 points for each treasure you find.)

1
FIND THE NORTH CAROLINA/TENNESSEE
State Boundary Line!
(Located at Newfound Gap)

SPECIAL HINT: Up until the 1850s there was another "gap" or route over the Smokies called "Indian Gap." Then guess what? Someone discovered this better "new found gap." Some describe this location as the centerpoint of the Smokies. About half the Great Smoky Mountains National Park is in Tennessee; the other half is in North Carolina. When was the last time you had the opportunity to straddle two states?

10 POINTS

2

STAND IN THE SHOES of
President Franklin D. Roosevelt!

(Use the display board as a guide.)

SPECIAL HINT: Stand in the exact spot where FDR dedicated the Great Smoky Mountains National Park in a ceremony on September 2, 1940. Thousands of people once lived in what is now the national park. The people of Tennessee and North Carolina raised about half the money ($5 million) to buy the land from private owners and businesses so that it could become a park. Even the schoolchildren saved their pennies to help. John D. Rockefeller, a wealthy busi-nessman, took care of the other half.

10 POINTS

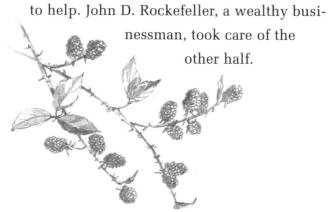

3

FIND OUT HOW MANY STATES
the Appalachian Trail (AT) Runs Through!

(Look near the trailhead.)

SPECIAL HINT: You are about to hike on one of the most
famous trails in the world! About 70 miles of the AT runs
through this national park. Most of the trail is
deep in the wilderness and not easily accessible.
Make sure your shoestrings are tied! **10 POINTS**

4

FIND THE WHITE BLAZE!

(As you head up the trail, look on the trees to the right.)

SPECIAL HINT: Whether in Maine or Georgia or in-between, the
painted white rectangle is the symbol that you are not lost—you
are on the AT! For 2,175 miles you will be
guided by the "white blaze." Today the blaze will
guide you all the way to Charlie's Bunion! **10 POINTS**

5

FIND THE DEAD FOREST of Fraser Fir Trees!

(Look on both sides of the trail at the first 90-degree left turn.)

SPECIAL HINT: The balsam woolly adelgid (*a-
DELL-jid*) insect came to the United States

from Europe about 100 years ago and showed up in the Smokies in 1963. These tiny insects killed thousands of mature Fraser fir trees throughout the park! You will walk directly under a dead Fraser fir tree up ahead. Such a powerful tree brought down by such tiny insects! Tens of thousands of insects infested and sucked the sap and the life out of each tree.

10 POINTS

6
FIND THE COMBINATION ROCK RAIN COVER and Rest Break Area!
(After you climb a rocky hill, search on the right.)

SPECIAL HINT: This small cavelike opening is a perfect spot to duck out of the rain or just take a load off! Hey! Any sign you're still on the AT?

10 POINTS

7
FIND THE NEWFOUND GAP ROAD!
(100 steps past the cavelike opening as the trail levels a bit— look toward North Carolina to your right.)

SPECIAL HINT: The road is located *out and down!* This road twists and turns its way from Gatlinburg, Tennessee, to Cherokee, North Carolina. Unless you want to drive about a "billion" miles, it is the only way to get between these two cities. This is the only road in the park that cuts across the mountains.

10 POINTS

Put your book away until you reach the intersection with Sweat Heifer Creek Trail at 1.7 miles. Settlers brought their cows up this trail to graze. You know it is steep with a name like "Sweat Heifer."

8
FIND THE HIDDEN POSTCARD VIEW
of North Carolina!
(Located on Sweat Heifer Creek Trail. Go
70 steps from the sign for the trail.)

SPECIAL HINT: Get off the AT at this intersection (Mile 1.7) and go right on Sweat Heifer Creek Trail heading toward Kephart Shelter. Go 70 paces from the sign at the intersection with the AT and you will find a rough opening for a private rest break with a view that will *knock your hiking socks off!* After your break, ***DON'T FORGET TO GET BACK ON THE AT!*** Turn right onto the AT.

10 POINTS

9
FIND THE LONG AND WINDING ROAD!
(As you head up a steep grade, take the short 8-foot-long
side path to the right of the AT.)

SPECIAL HINT: Look for the Newfound Gap Road switching back and forth around a huge mountain. You can see the entire switch-back from this spot! The Cherokee word "Shaconage" (*shuh-KON-a-gee*) means "the land of blue smoke." The blue haze is caused by "zillions" of plants and trees releasing vapor into the air.

10 POINTS

10
FIND CLINGMAN'S DOME
Ramp and Observation Tower!
(Located across—south and right—
from the rocky clearing near the top of the ridge)

SPECIAL HINT: This is an incredible view of layers upon layers of mountain ridges! At 6,643 feet, **Clingman's Dome is the highest peak in the park!** Look southwest to the highest mountain range in the distance. On a clear day you can see the outline of the tower. If you don't have a compass, just look out yonder to your far right. Binoculars or someone related to an eagle would be a good thing to have on hand at this juncture!

10 POINTS

11
FIND THE SPRUCE FIR FOREST!
(Hike awhile—then search on both sides of the
trail as you finally begin to head down the slope.
Thank goodness for downhill!)

SPECIAL HINT: You are walking through a forest of red spruce and Fraser fir trees. Red spruce have very short needles that are pointed and sharp. The needles are about an inch long. A Fraser fir tree's needles are longer, flat, and are whitish on the underside. You could conduct a scientific test by touching the ends of the needles. If it hurts, it is probably a red spruce. If it doesn't hurt at all, it is probably a Fraser fir. Thank goodness for science!

SPECIAL NOTE: Between the spruce fir forest and Icewater Spring is a log on the left of the trail that was *hot-iron branded* with the AT symbol! Pretty cool if you find it.

◯

10 POINTS

12

FIND THE "MILLION FEET GULLEY"!

(Hike awhile—bear right toward Charlie's Bunion at the intersection with the Boulevard Trail at Mile 2.7. The Boulevard Trail leads to Mount LeConte . . . not today, folks!)

SPECIAL HINT: Hike downhill for a few minutes and notice the deep gully. This gully was created by millions of **hikers like you** trodding down on the mud and dirt. It keeps getting deeper and deeper!

◯

10 POINTS

13

FIND ICEWATER SPRING BACKCOUNTRY SHELTER!

(About a quarter mile past the intersection with the Boulevard Trail)

SPECIAL HINT: Look for the narrow path to the right. It will lead to the shelter. Find the shelter's fireplace and unique "privy" (a restroom facility in the middle of the wilderness). There are about 15 backcountry shelters in the park for use by backpackers. A lot of folks who stay in this shelter are hiking on the AT all the way from Maine to Georgia, or from Georgia to Maine! They are called "thru-hikers." There is a guest book for comments by those who sleep in the shelter. Take a look! Very interesting!

◯

10 POINTS

14

FIND THE BEAR AVOIDANCE
Food Pulley and Hoist System!

(Located near the Icewater Spring Shelter)

SPECIAL HINT: Look for a wire and pulley system between two trees that hikers use to hoist up their backpacks and food so bears cannot get to them. Bears are also attracted to toothpaste, hairspray, and shaving cream! *You don't want nothin' that smells in that shelter!* There are about 1,500 black bears walking around in this park. It's been said that a bear can climb *up* a tree faster than you can fall out of one!

10 POINTS

15

FIND SIGNS OF WILD HOGS!

(Explore around the Icewater Spring Shelter and farther up the Appalachian Trail.)

SPECIAL HINT: Look for areas on the ground that wild hogs rooted up with their snouts to find acorns and plants to eat. Wild hogs also eat snakes, snails, small mammals, salamanders, and bird eggs and can weigh up to 300 pounds. Some park rangers are employed *full-time* to hunt for hogs. The hogs are not native to the park, and they destroy plants, pollute the streams, and eat animals that are native to the park. In the 1940s someone had a bad idea to bring some wild boars from Europe to a game preserve in North Carolina. They got loose and bred with farmers' pigs in the Smokies. More than 10,000 of them have been removed from the park since then. Hundreds still roam the park at night!

10 POINTS

16

FIND THE ICEWATER SPRING!

(As you leave the shelter and go right onto the AT, look for a metal pipe in a small stream of water crossing the trail.)

SPECIAL HINT: This is a very high-elevation spring, and the water is really cold. Some say it is as cold as _ _ _ _ _ _ _ _!

10 POINTS

Put your book away for the final mile to Charlie's Bunion.

17

FIND CHARLIE'S BUNION!

(The Appalachian Trail has a Bunion Bypass to the right as you approach the Bunion. Bear to the left when you reach that split in the trail—you're only 100 yards from the bunion! Yes!)

SPECIAL HINT: A fire in 1925 burned off all the vegetation on Charlie's Bunion. Four years later, a heavy rain washed off all the roots on this rocky pinnacle. Horace Kephart, a writer and park supporter, asked George Masa, a photographer, and **Charlie Conner,** a local mountaineer, to help him survey the damage. Charlie's foot was hurting by the time they reached the rock vista, and later when Kephart sat on a special committee to name places in the park, he suggested naming this pinnacle "Charlie's Bunion." Conner later said that he never really had a bunion. We applaud Kephart, because we think "Charlie's Bunion" is a much better name than "Charlie's Achin' Foot"!

○

10 POINTS

18
FIND MOUNT LECONTE!
(Look northwest, left, of Charlie's Achin' Foot
—I mean Charlie's Bunion.)

SPECIAL HINT: Look across the valley from Charlie's Bunion, an incredible sheer drop with a very scenic pinnacle. Look for the mountain that has great scars (stripped area, brownish in color) to find Mount LeConte, the third highest peak in the park. A flash flood on Labor Day weekend in 1951 tore off vegetation on the north slope of Mount LeConte. The only resort lodging in the park is on top of that mountain! The food is brought to the lodge on the backs of llamas! Wouldn't it be nice if llamas showed up *right now* with fried chicken, potato salad, ice-cold sweet tea, and pineapple upside-down cake? Oh, well . . . pass the trail mix, please.

○

10 POINTS

19
FIND MASA KNOB!

(Look for the rock peak right before
you reached Charlie's Bunion.)

SPECIAL HINT: Remember the name of the photographer in Kephart's group in Clue #17? Just think. If Kephart would have asked *you* to come along to survey the damage, this pinnacle might have been named for you!

How are your feet?

◯

10 POINTS

CONGRATULATIONS!

You have just completed a

Great Smoky Mountains National Park

Scavenger Hike Adventure!

Appalachian Trail to Charlie's Bunion

10 points for each item found

Total Score _____

Certified Achievement Level _____

50 to 100 points: *City Slicker*

Over **100 to 130** points: *Pioneer Scout*

Over **130** points: *Frontier Explorer*

Name(s): _____

_____

Witness(es) thereof: _____

_____

Date: _____

Journal Notes

The people on this hike were:

_____

_____

_____

_____

The weather was:

_____

_____

_____

_____

We saw:

_____

_____

_____

_____

More about our adventure:

_____

_____

_____

_____

_____

Scavenger Hike Adventure

Trillium Gap Trail to Grotto Falls

WHY THIS IS A GREAT TRAIL! This Scavenger Hike Adventure is on a beautiful trail with giant trees that are hundreds of years old! The trail leads to an incredible waterfall with a 25-foot drop. You will find a crystal-clear pool of water at the bottom of the falls. You can walk *right behind* Grotto Falls! You will search for salamanders in some great places to find them! Keep your eyes wide open, because this is the only trail in the park where you just might see a **llama!** Llamas use this trail to carry supplies up to the rustic lodge at the top of Mount LeConte. You will be hiking along one of the steepest streams in the park (Roaring Fork), with water tumbling all the way down from Mount LeConte over a half mile above you! You'll find a few streams that you must cross with no footbridges! Happy rock hopping!

WHERE'S THE TRAIL? From the Sugarlands Visitor Center go north on U.S. Highway 441 into Gatlinburg. Turn right (east) at **Stoplight #8,** Historic Nature Trail/Airport Road (stoplights are all numbered in Gatlinburg). Follow the signs to the **Roaring Fork Motor Nature Trail.** The Trillium Gap trailhead, which leads to Grotto Falls, is at Marker #5 on the motor trail. It is well marked by a sign.

ABOUT THE TRAIL: This MODERATE hike follows a sloped, wide dirt trail. Grotto Falls is *well hiked* and *well liked!* A bonus on this Scavenger Hike Adventure is that to get to the trailhead you must travel on the **Roaring Fork Motor Nature Trail!** This one-way, narrow 5-mile loop through dense forests passes many beautiful streams and restored cabins. It can best be described as a "mountain hike" for your car! Your car will absolutely love it! This road is closed in the winter months.

HOW LONG IS THIS HIKE? This Scavenger Hike Adventure is about 3 miles round-trip. You should allow a couple of hours for this hike.

SPECIAL COMMENT: If you continue on past Grotto Falls for another 1.7 miles, you will reach a beautiful "heath bald" on top of **Brushy Mountain.** A heath bald is an area covered with shrubs from the heath family such as catawba rhododendron, mountain laurel, and sand myrtle. Trees seldom grow there because of the thin soil and harsh environment at the higher elevations. Narrow paths cut through the heath bald and lead to some of the most awesome views you'll ever see! You will feel like you are standing on top of the world! It is pretty steep to get there, so if you are huffin' and puffin' at the falls, you may want to go on back down the hill. If you ain't huffin'— don't miss the pinnacle views from the top of Brushy Mountain! The views will take your breath away—if the hike up hasn't already!

THINGS TO HUNT FOR

(Earn 10 points for each treasure you find.)

1

FIND A PAVED CORNFIELD!

(As you park your vehicle)

SPECIAL HINT: This parking lot was once an open field of corn! In fact, the road you traveled on to get here, **Roaring Fork Motor Nature Trail,** was once a rough wagon trail leading to Gatlinburg. The Roaring Fork community was settled about 160 years ago. In the early 1900s about two dozen families made Roaring Fork their home. My, how times do change!

10 POINTS

2

FIND A BIG . . . No, I Mean Huge . . . No, I Really Mean . . . *Gargantuan* HEMLOCK TREE!

(Head up the trail. Look on the right side of the trail—
so close you could touch it with a hiking stick.)

SPECIAL HINT: Look for dark-reddish-brown bark on a huge tree with branches of needles that some folks think look lacy! To know for sure that you found the correct tree, look for a boulder at the base of the tree with a little skinny stripe of white quartz rock running through it. You are standing in an old-growth forest! That means that this part of the forest wasn't logged or farmed. Some of the humongous trees along this trail are hundreds of years old! Some of the trees in old-growth forests in the Smokies are over 500 years old!

10 POINTS

3

FIND THE TREE
Growing on a Flat Plate of Rock!

(Go 17 steps from that *gargantuan* tree you just found—search on the right.)

SPECIAL HINT: Trees somehow just manage to deal with all the millions of rocks in the Smoky Mountains! Tree roots sometimes break right through rocks to search for food and water! You'll see more examples up ahead on the right. These trees let nothing stop them. They just "Rock On"!

10 POINTS

4
FIND A LLAMA TRAIL!

(Go up the hill and find the sign for
TRILLIUM GAP TRAIL—head toward Grotto Falls.)

SPECIAL HINT: Trillium Gap Trail leads llamas and people to a rustic resort over a half-mile above you at the top of Mount LeConte. You can make a reservation and hike up there and spend the night. Llamas will bring you a great dinner and breakfast! They carry the food and clean sheets and pillow-cases on their backs! Llama hooves are padded and smaller than horses' hooves and cause much less dam- age to the trail. Keep your eyes wide open. You just might see a llama!

10 POINTS

5
FIND THE WILD AND CRAZY BROWN WOODY GRAPEVINES!

(Cross the stream—count 65 steps past the
stream—search on the left.)

SPECIAL HINT: Look up at the wild and crazy woody grapevines climbing this way and that way all over the trees! Opossums, skunks, bears, and other critters in the Smokies enjoy eating the sour wild grapes. Long ago, Cherokee Indians who lived in this area believed that burning grapevine wood and oak together would bring a spell of warm weather in the middle of a cold winter!

10 POINTS

6

FIND A "ZILLION" FERNS!

(After a sharp right turn in the trail—walk about
1 minute and look on the mountainside.)

SPECIAL HINT: These **ladyferns** have very dainty leaves that
are delicate and look like green lace. This fern is beautiful, and
there are "zillions" of them all along this trail.
Many different types of ferns grow in both moist
and dry environments in the Smoky Mountains.　**10 POINTS**

7

FIND A SIGN OF A BEAR!

(Look all along the trail—but be careful that you don't miss #8.)

SPECIAL HINT: Look for signs of bears all along the trail! Search
for logs or lower portions of trees that have been clawed, ripped
apart, or shredded by bears looking for termites, grubs, and other
insects to eat. There are many examples along the trail. There are
about two black bears for every square mile in this
park (about 1,500 bears in total). *Go on to #8 as
you keep your eyes wide open for signs of bears!*　**10 POINTS**

8

FIND A TALL TREE STUMP
That Used to Bend over the "Holler" with Hundreds
of Shoots Growing Up from the Base!

(It will take a little while to get to this tree—look on
the left as the trail heads uphill and bends to the right.)

SPECIAL HINT: Hundreds of little shoots are growing at the base of the trunk. This is a **basswood tree!** It has heart-shaped leaves. The tall tree used to bend over the holler, and you can find the rest of the tree on the ground. Bees swarm the yellow flowers of basswood when they bloom in early summer. Basswood honey was a favorite of mountain folks. Cherokee Indians and others used the basswood for carving. Pioneers would hollow out basswood logs to make barrels.　**10 POINTS**

9
FIND A BEAR MATTRESS!
(Stand at the edge of the small stream that crosses the trail— look on the right and back behind you.)

SPECIAL HINT: These shrubs are found all throughout the park. Their long, thick, and narrow leaves are evergreen. Rhododendrons have beautiful flowers in late spring and early summer! Bears sometimes gather the branches of leaves to use for bedding in winter dens. ***Remember, don't take anything or pick anything or leave anything! In other words, protect this awesome place!***　**10 POINTS**

10
FIND A PARTRIDGE BERRY, Not in a Pear Tree!
(Located on the hillside near the right side of the trail)

SPECIAL HINT: This partridge berry plant grows low to the ground and has tiny dark-green leaves with a very noticeable white vein in the middle of each leaf. To get the points, you must find a red berry or a white blossom! Look all along the mountain-side as you continue toward the falls. *Be "berry"* *careful to protect the berries and every plant in* *this park. Please leave them for all to see!* ◯ **10 POINTS**

11

FIND THE "BIG BIRD" BEAK!

(Hike awhile—cross another stream—then pass a huge hemlock
tree in the middle of the trail with big roots and
clear paths going around the tree on the left and the right.
Then, up ahead, look on the left of the trail.)

SPECIAL HINT: Look for the huge boulder pointing to the sky
like a bird looking up toward the sun. This rock
formation looks like a **bird head and beak!** Use ◯
your imagination and find this rock bird! **10 POINTS**

12

FIND THE LOW SHRUBS with Sharp-edged Leaves!

(15 steps past the "big bird" beak—
search on the left of the trail.)

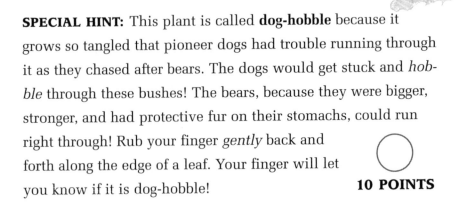

SPECIAL HINT: This plant is called **dog-hobble** because it
grows so tangled that pioneer dogs had trouble running through
it as they chased after bears. The dogs would get stuck and *hob-ble* through these bushes! The bears, because they were bigger,
stronger, and had protective fur on their stomachs, could run
right through! Rub your finger *gently* back and ◯
forth along the edge of a leaf. Your finger will let
you know if it is dog-hobble! **10 POINTS**

13

FIND THE QUARTZ "SANDWICH"!

(Located on the opposite side of the
trail from the dog-hobble)

SPECIAL HINT: Look for the rock with a strand
of **white quartz** running right through it! Looks
like a sandwich, eh? I bet it weighs more than a
quarter-pounder!

10 POINTS

14

LISTEN AND THEN FIND THE CASCADES and Waterfall That Are *Not* Grotto Falls!

(Cross a stream—search down in the holler on the left.)

SPECIAL HINT: This is beautiful, but is *not* the waterfall you
are searching for! Keep going! You are almost there! The stream
below you, **Roaring Fork,** is falling all the way from Mount
LeConte (more than a mile high in elevation). It is likely the
steepest stream in the Smoky Mountains! The
water gets pretty noisy as it rushes down the
mountain. Sounds kind of like a "roar"!

10 POINTS

15

FIND GROTTO FALLS!

(In front of you)

SPECIAL HINT: Listen for someone to say, "Whoa! Jiminy
Crickets! Wow! There it is!" (or something like that). There is a

large pool at the base of the falls that is a perfect spot to cool off your feet on a hot day.

16

WALK BEHIND GROTTO FALLS!

(Carefully follow the trail that leads behind the falls.)

SPECIAL HINT: If you wish to get all wet, you will never have a better opportunity! This is called *Grotto* Falls because of the cavelike opening behind the falls. ("Grotto" is another word for cave.)

10 POINTS

17

FIND A SALAMANDER!

(Look around the base of the falls.)

SPECIAL HINT: Look under rocks and around the edges of the pool of water. Salamanders in the park grow from ½ inch to more than 2 feet long! There are 31 different kinds of salamanders in all colors and sizes living in the park! Some folks call the Smokies the "Salamander Capital of the World"! Can you find just one? If you do find one, treat it gently, and don't keep it out of the water for more than a minute. A salamander's skin can dry out very quickly!

10 POINTS

CONGRATULATIONS!

You have just completed a

Great Smoky Mountains National Park

Scavenger Hike Adventure!

Trillium Gap Trail to Grotto Falls

10 points for each item found

Total Score _____

Certified Achievement Level _____

50 to 100 points: *City Slicker*

Over **100 to 140** points: *Pioneer Scout*

Over **140** points: *Frontier Explorer*

Name(s): _____

_____

Witness(es) thereof: _____

Date: _____

Journal Notes

The people on this hike were:
_____

_____

_____

_____

The weather was:
_____

_____

_____

_____

We saw:
_____

_____

_____

_____

More about our adventure:
_____

_____

_____

_____

Scavenger Hike Adventure

6

Big Creek Trail to Midnight Hole
and Mouse Creek Falls

WHY THIS IS A GREAT TRAIL! This Scavenger Hike
Adventure is located in Big Creek, an area of the park **off the
beaten path.** If you want wilderness—oh, brother, this is it!
You will find some of the most awesome white-water mountain
stream views in the park! Someone very smart named this Big
Creek because . . . this is a *really* big creek! On this trail you
will find boulders the size of FIVE CAMPING TRAILERS
stacked on top of one
another! Find the huge
Rock House up on a
hill! Find the
"Midnight Hole," a
deep dark pool fed by
beautiful cascading water
squeezed between huge boulders! Sun

the trees in this area and now new trees have grown back. That is why it is called a **second-growth** forest.

10 POINTS

2
FIND THE SPECIAL BEAR-PROOF GARBAGE CAN!
(Located in the parking lot)

SPECIAL HINT: There are about 1,500 black bears in the park! This special garbage can is built so that a bear can't put his paw in it to get food. Check it out! If bears eat people food, they'll get into trouble looking for food in all the wrong places! *Never* feed a bear, because it will lose its wild instincts and become "habituated," which means it loses its fear of people. That is not a good thing for it or us! Bears that are not afraid of humans may become "nuisance" bears and often have to be removed from the park or sometimes killed. *So please don't feed the bears!*

10 POINTS

3
FIND THE FURRY VINE
Climbing up the "Triplet" Tulip Tree!
(At the corner of the parking area near a
huge sawed-off tree trunk)

SPECIAL HINT: This tulip tree is joined at the bottom but then splits into three trunks and looks sort of like a "triplet" tree. The furry vine climbing up the tree is **poison ivy!** Poison ivy has groups of three leaves and grows on the ground, but it occasionally just attaches to a tree and heads to the sky! Leaves of three, let it be! Furry vine, you'll itch and whine! Do not touch the vine or the leaves. Hiking and itching like crazy at the same time is not a good thing! You'll see a few more huge, furry poison ivy vines on the left as you head up the trail.

10 POINTS

4
FIND THE CHRISTMAS FERNS!
(On the right—near the beginning of the trail)

SPECIAL HINT: The folks that named this evergreen fern thought that the individual leaves were shaped like Santa's sleigh or maybe a Christmas stocking. What do you think? If you're hiking in December, Merry Christmas and Happy Holidays to all!

10 POINTS

5

FIND HUNDREDS OF PENCIL TREES!
(On the left as you look toward the creek)

SPECIAL HINT: As you continue on the trail and look to the left, you can't help but notice the hundreds of extremely tall and straight **tulip trees** (also called yellow poplars). They look like giant pencils! This area was cleared by loggers in the early 1900s, and with all the trees gone, the sun shined brightly down below you. The tulip tree seedlings absolutely loved it! You are looking at a huge "stand" of tulip trees. Throughout the park, when you see a group of trees like this, it indicates that the land was probably once cleared by either loggers or farmers.

10 POINTS

6

FIND THE AWESOME STRATIFIED SANDSTONE FORMATION!

(On the mountainside—on the right of the trail.
After you see the creek flowing close by the trail, start looking.)

SPECIAL HINT: Some of the rocks look like **shingles** sticking out from the side of the mountain. The thin layers of rock sometimes rise about 50 feet along this trail! Just look for the layered rocks that run along the trail for about a quarter of a mile. It is quite awesome!

10 POINTS

7

FIND AMAZING TREES Growing Right Out of a Boulder the Size of a Schoolbus!

(Look up and into the forest on the right.)

SPECIAL HINT: There are three trees growing out of a boulder the size of a school bus!

10 POINTS

8

FIND THOUSANDS OF HUGE BOULDERS
Strewn on the Mountainside!

(Hike 10 to 15 minutes—search on the right side of the
trail on the side of the mountain.)

SPECIAL HINT: Due to freezing and thawing, these rocks
cracked and broke off from the mountain and then tumbled
on down! Geologists call large groups of boulders, such as
you see here, a **block field.** You'll see thousands of boulders
in this block field! Scientists believe some rocks in the
Smokies are about 600 million years old. The boulders on this
trail are so huge and awesome that when you see them, they
just might knock your hiking socks off! If you
are not sure that you have found the block field
. . . YOU HAVEN'T!

10 POINTS

9

FIND A BOULDER as Big as a Winnebago!

(On the right side of the trail—you could touch it with a
hiking stick without stepping off the trail.)

SPECIAL HINT: If this had wheels, windows,
and an engine, you could use it
as an RV!

10 POINTS

10

FIND THE ROCK HOUSE in the Sky!

(On the right side of the trail—way up high among the trees.
Start looking when Big Creek gets very close to the trail and
you see a lot of boulders the size of small cars in the creek.)

SPECIAL HINT: This is likely the most unusual boulder you've
ever seen in your life! You have seen some *huge* boulders on
this trail, but this one is AT LEAST TWICE AS BIG as the
biggest one you've seen so far! It looks more like a house than a
boulder! ***A narrow, steep, almost-hidden footpath*** leads up to
the **Rock House!** It has three walls and a ceiling,
and loggers would use it to get in out of bad
weather.   **10 POINTS**

11

FIND THE WALL OF RHODODENDRON BUSHES!

(Located on the right side of the trail—all along the way)

SPECIAL HINT: The leaves of these plants are long and slen-
der and are green year-round. The leaves are really thick and
feel like leather, and the bushes are full of beautiful blossoms
in the summer. Cherokee Indians once lived in this area. They
would not burn rhododendron wood or leaves because they
believed it would bring cold winter weather.
The burning wood and leaves would hiss and
sound like a windy snowstorm!   **10 POINTS**

12

FIND THE AWESOME "MIDNIGHT HOLE"!

(Hike awhile—look on the left side of the trail down in the creek when you find a *wide-open rocky clearing.*)

SPECIAL HINT: As you walk along, look for a dark, deep pool of water fed by waterfalls that rush **between large boulders** in the middle of the creek. When the water is high, there will be one waterfall. When the water is lower, you will see two waterfalls plummeting over the rocks. There is a wide opening and a well-worn path leading down to **Midnight Hole.** The pool is dark green in the winter and midnight blue in the summer. This is an awesome spot for sunning and picnicking! Take off your shoes and rest a spell! It doesn't get any better than this!

10 POINTS

13

FIND A TROUT!

(In Midnight Hole)

SPECIAL HINT: Trout like to hang out in Midnight Hole. Look carefully and you may be able to spot one. There are 2,000 to 4,000 trout per mile in some of the streams in the park! During

the middle of the day, trout usually rest near the bottom, so cup your eyes and peer deeply into the hole. One local old-timer comes up here every week to fish for a couple of meals!

10 POINTS

14

FIND THE ROCK WALL That Holds Up the Trail!

(Near Midnight Hole—alongside the trail)

SPECIAL HINT: As you return to the trail from Midnight Hole, look for the rock wall that supports the trail. Big Creek Trail was once an Indian path! In the early 1900s loggers used the trail as a logging road! In the 1930s it became an automobile road for the men who were building the trails in the park! Now Big Creek Trail is a trail for people and horses!

10 POINTS

15

FIND THE HUMONGOUS BOULDER That Looks like a House with a Green Roof and Green Trim!

(On the right side of the trail—
behind some rhododendron bushes)

SPECIAL HINT: This boulder stands alone and is about the size of a two-story house! This giant "pebble" is covered with soft green moss! It almost looks like a house with a green roof!

10 POINTS

16

FIND THE HITCHING POSTS for Horses!

(On the left side of the trail—near a wide-open area)

SPECIAL HINT: Tie up your horses (or anyone who asked, "Are we almost there yet?") and mosey on over to **Mouse Creek Falls!**

10 POINTS

17

FIND MOUSE CREEK FALLS!

(Just a few feet upstream from the hitching posts)

SPECIAL HINT: Find the beautiful cascading waterfall that drops 50 feet to Mouse Creek! There used to be railroad tracks used for logging at the base of the falls. The railroad line was located right where the water first hits the flat area. Listen! You *won't* hear the sound of a train engine chugging along with black smoke pumping out of the stack. Today you will hear only the peaceful sounds of nature as the crystal-clear mountain water tumbles from the high slopes of Mount Sterling.

$\bigcirc$

10 POINTS

BONUS COURTESY HINT: If you didn't find the **Rock House** and want to try *one more time*—it is located about 550 steps heading back from the side path leading to Midnight Hole.

CONGRATULATIONS!

You have just completed a

Great Smoky Mountains National Park

Scavenger Hike Adventure!

Big Creek Trail to Midnight Hole and Mouse Creek Falls

10 points for each item found

Total Score _____

Certified Achievement Level _____

50 to 100 points:

City Slicker

Over **100 to 140** points:

Pioneer Scout

Over **140** points:

Frontier Explorer

Name(s): _____

_____

Witness(es) thereof: _____

Date: _____

Journal Notes

The people on this hike were:

_____

_____

_____

_____

The weather was:

_____

_____

_____

_____

We saw:

_____

_____

_____

_____

More about our adventure:

_____

_____

_____

_____

_____

Scavenger Hike Adventure

Sugarlands Valley Nature Trail

WHY THIS IS A GREAT TRAIL! This is an *easy and exciting* Scavenger Hike Adventure through a deep green forest along a beautiful mountain stream! You will find the actual foot-path Cherokee Indians walked on to get to North Carolina a long, long time ago! A whole community of pioneers lived in this **Sugarlands** area, which was named for all the sugar maple trees that used to be here! One thing for sure, these pioneers had *plenty* of maple syrup! A black bear liked this trail so much it couldn't *bear* to wait for the wet cement to dry! Find the paw prints! Be cool! You can dip your feet in a mountain stream! This trail is great for everyone!

WHERE'S THE TRAIL? From the Sugarlands Visitor Center (an awesome place to visit!), this trail is about a 2-minute (less than a half-mile) drive south on U.S. Highway 441 toward Newfound Gap and Cherokee, North Carolina. It is so close, there is not even time for anyone to ask, "Are we there yet?" Look on the right side of the road for the sign SUGARLANDS VALLEY NATURE TRAIL. Parking and the trail will be across from the sign on the left side of the road.

ABOUT THE TRAIL: This paved trail is wide and level and great for wheelchairs and strollers. It is almost totally shaded because it goes through a thick forest. Many benches along the way make it easy to take this EASY hike!

HOW LONG IS THIS HIKE? This Scavenger Hike Adventure is about a half-mile loop and will take less than an hour to complete!

THINGS TO HUNT FOR

(Earn 10 points for each treasure you find.)

1
FIND A BIG ROCK
with Two Holes Shaped like Eyes!
(On the right—near start of the trail)

SPECIAL HINT: Use your imagination! Does it look like anyone in *your* family? How did nature make those holes? Most likely these holes were made by water swirling on the rock for millions of years! Swirling waters can make rocks round and smooth like this one. Fast-moving streams carry stones, logs, and grains of sand that can make cracks, holes, and marks on the rocks. This rock isn't quite ready to be placed on Mount Rushmore, but it *is* an interesting "face"!

10 POINTS

2

FIND A TREE That Looks More like a "Twin" Tree!
(About 10 steps before reaching
the footbridge—on the right of the trail)

SPECIAL HINT: Nature is *amazing!* The trunk of this tree was somehow split and has grown into *two* trunks! When this tree was very young, it definitely experienced some sort of trauma! Maybe it was struck by lightning, chewed on by an animal, or damaged by strong winds. *Something* caused the trunk to grow into twin twunks and to grow into what now looks like a "twin twee"!

10 POINTS

3

FIND THE NUMBER OF FAMILIES
That Once Lived in the Sugarlands Valley!
(At Marker #1)

SPECIAL HINT: Check out this sign! Indians walked on this land prior to white settlers! Pioneers came here more than 150 years ago, and life was not easy for them! They had to work hard to survive! The Smoky Mountains is a very rocky place, and pioneers had to move thousands of heavy rocks to clear this land so they could plant crops and raise their own animals for food! Where you are now standing was once a community with three schools, a post office, two churches, two tub mills, a sawmill, farm fields, and many homesteads! Just think, people lived here when Abraham Lincoln was president!

10 POINTS

4

FIND A LARGE STONE CHIMNEY
and a Fireplace!
(On the left of the trail)

SPECIAL HINT: This fireplace and chimney were built about 100 years ago! What you see is all that is left of a family's summer vacation home! People built vacation homes in the Smokies as early as 1900. In the early 1930s Congress decided to make the Smoky Mountains into a national park, so all the land in this area was bought from private owners. Imagine sitting by this fireplace way back then! People loved to vacation in the Smokies! I guess *some* things *never* change! **10 POINTS**

5
SPOT A ROCK (BOULDER)
That Weighs More than You!

(On the left of the trail—right past the bench
—down in the stream)

SPECIAL HINT: There are lots of humongous and very heavy boulders in the Smoky Mountains! How in the world did all of these huge rocks get here? At one time the Smoky Mountains were much higher than they are today! These mountains once were even taller than the Rocky Mountains! During a much colder era, water froze in cracks in the mountain rock. When it froze, it expanded and broke the rock! Gravity and fast-moving rivers and streams then carried these huge boulders down the mountains to where they are today! In the Smokies there are boulders, boulders, everywhere!

10 POINTS

6
FIND THE REMAINS OF ANOTHER
SMOKY MOUNTAIN VACATION HOME!

(On the right of the trail)

SPECIAL HINT: This fireplace has **white quartz** rocks built into the front of the stonework. We'll never know why the builder decided to put them there. Maybe the stones had some special meaning to him. Take a look! Quartz is a very common rock in the Smokies and is often milky white.

10 POINTS

TAKE ONLY PICTURES—LEAVE ONLY FOOTPRINTS

7

FIND THE SOFT, BEAUTIFUL HEMLOCK TREES!

(Surrounding the chimney and fireplace)

SPECIAL HINT: Hemlock trees have short, flat needles. Some describe these beautiful branches of needles as "lacy." Hemlocks have very tiny cones. Gently rub the needles between your fingers and take a "whiff." Now, when someone asks, "What did you do today?" say, "I smelled a hemlock!" A tiny insect from Asia called the hemlock woolly adelgid (*a-DELL-jid*) is attacking our hemlocks. Park rangers are doing all that they can do to save these beautiful trees.

10 POINTS

8

FIND UMBRELLAS OVER YOUR HEAD!

(About 46 steps past the chimney)

SPECIAL HINT: Look straight up! Find the leaves of the umbrella magnolia tree! Umbrellas sure come in handy in the Smokies because it rains a lot here! It rains more in the Smokies than in almost any other place in the United States! In fact, it rains more than 7 feet each year in the higher elevations! This is one of the reasons the Smokies is such a special place! "Zillions"

of plants and animals live here! There are more kinds of trees than in any other area of the same size in the whole United States! There are more flowering plants than in any other national park in our country! The *diversity* of life in the Smokies is incredible! (Natural umbrellas are not available in winter and early spring.) **10 POINTS**

9
FIND A TREE That Looks like It's Wearing a Shoe!
(On the left of the trail—past the bench)

SPECIAL HINT: This tree trunk looks just like a very long leg that is wearing a **shoe made of rock!** Nature has a great sense of humor!

10
FIND THE OLD CHEROKEE FOOTPATH!
(At Marker #3—in the gully—near the stream)

SPECIAL HINT: Stand in the **gully** between Marker #3 and the stream! You are actually standing on an old Indian path where Cherokee Indians walked all the way to North Carolina many years ago! Imagine Indians walking down this footpath! Many Cherokee lived in the area of the Smoky Mountains long ago, and many still live across the mountains in Cherokee, North Carolina, on the Qualla Indian Reservation! **10 POINTS**

can put your fingers in the grooves of this tree's thick bark! The bark almost looks like the tread on the tires of your car. Mountain folks seldom chopped down sourwood trees to use for fuel because they loved the honey the bees made from its flowers! You can buy sourwood honey in town. Try it! You'll like it!

10 POINTS

16
FIND THE BABY BIRDS
with a Mother Bird!

(Walk awhile—on the right side of the trail.)

SPECIAL HINT: Look closely and see how many baby birds are waiting to be fed by their mother! Indians, pioneers, vacationers, and lots of critters have all come to the Sugarlands Valley. Many animals now make the Smokies their home! In the Smokies, birds are more often heard than seen because they are hidden in the thick forests of trees and plants. More than 240 species of birds have been recorded in the Great Smoky Mountains National Park. The largest bird that lives here is the wild turkey! Hope you see one! It is an awesome bird!

10 POINTS

17
FIND THE DOG-HOBBLE!

(On the left of the trail—across from a rock wall)

SPECIAL HINT: This low evergreen plant has sharp edges on its leaves. Rub your finger gently back and forth across the edge of a leaf! These tangled bushes are called **dog-hobble.** A long time ago, dogs would get tangled up in these low bushes while they were chasing after bears. I guess you could say these bushes could really make a dog hobble! The bigger, stronger bears would just glide right through the dog-hobble! Dog-hobble grows only in the Southern Appalachian Mountains. Some of the leaves turn bronze, maroon, and copper in the fall and winter.

10 POINTS

18

FIND POISON IVY Climbing up a Tree!

(Find the POISON IVY sign—on the right of the trail.
Look ahead for a vine climbing up a tree.)

SPECIAL HINT: This furry vine is poison ivy! Don't touch it! It will make you itch! Poison ivy can also come in the form of three green leaves. Remember: Leaves of three, let it be! Furry vine, you'll itch and whine! It is not uncommon to find poison ivy vines as thick as your arm climbing up the sides of large trees here in the Smokies! **10 POINTS**

19

JUST FOR FUN!

(Find the oldest person in your group and
speak to him or her in Cherokee!)

SPECIAL HINT: Say **"Shee-oh. Doh-huh-dun-nay?"** This is Cherokee for "Hi! How are you doing?" **Chief Sequoyah** first discovered that the spoken word could also be written down when he saw white settlers reading from a printed paper. He called the paper with words **"talking leaves."** Chief Sequoya wanted his people to have "talking leaves," so he spent the next 12 years writing symbols for each Cherokee syllable. On his own he developed the written Cherokee language. Today children in Cherokee, North Carolina, learn both English and the Cherokee language in their schools.

10 POINTS

20
FIND A TULIP TREE!

(On the right of the trail—about 42 steps past Marker #6— search on the right of the trail. A sign marks the spot.)

SPECIAL HINT: Look straight up! Today this forest is made up of many very tall **tulip trees.** A tulip tree is often a sign of where a cornfield used to be. Tulip trees grow up in sunny places, and since this area was once an open field and was also logged, there was certainly lots of sun! Tulip trees, also known as yellow poplars, were often *so large* that a pioneer family could build an entire cabin from just one tree!

10 POINTS

21
FIND THE PANCAKE SYRUP TREE!

(28 steps from the tulip tree—on the right)

SPECIAL HINT: Pioneers used the sap from the **sugar maple tree** to make delicious maple syrup. Pass the pancakes, please!

10 POINTS

CONGRATULATIONS!

You have just completed a

Great Smoky Mountains National Park

Scavenger Hike Adventure!

Sugarlands Valley Nature Trail

10 points for each item found

Total Score _____

Certified Achievement Level _____

50 to 100 points: *City Slicker*

Over **100 to 180** points: *Pioneer Scout*

Over **180** points: *Frontier Explorer*

Name(s): _____

_____

Witness(es) thereof: _____

Date: _____

Journal Notes

The people on this hike were:

_____

_____

_____

_____

The weather was:

_____

_____

_____

_____

We saw:

_____

_____

_____

_____

More about our adventure:

_____

_____

_____

_____

_____

Scavenger Hike Adventure

Cades Cove to Abrams Falls Trail
to Abrams Falls

WHY THIS IS A GREAT TRAIL! This Scavenger Hike Adventure begins in world-famous Cades Cove with a search for deer and bears on the way to the trailhead! Cades Cove is a beautiful valley surrounded by majestic mountains. Can you believe one visitor saw 200 deer on just one trip through Cades Cove! There have also been hundreds of sightings of bears up in cherry trees or meandering through these woods. This hiking trail follows Abrams Creek, the *biggest* stream that runs entirely within the boundaries of the park. You'll find a gargantuan white pine tree, the most hypnotic smooth cascade you've ever seen, more mountain laurel than you can shake a stick at, and finally powerful **Abrams Falls** crashing 25 feet into a huge, deep pool of water! This is a great place to cool off and picnic!

WHERE'S THE TRAIL? From Sugarlands Visitor Center follow the signs to Cades Cove. It's about 24 miles (about an hour's drive) on beautiful, winding Little River Road. Then follow the Cades Cove loop road for about 5 miles and turn right (just past Marker #10) onto the gravel road following the sign to the Abrams Falls trailhead.

ABOUT THE TRAIL: This is a wide and mostly level trail, but it has three or four pretty good hills to climb. The trail is sometimes dirt and pine needles, sometimes very rocky, and sometimes very "rooty." The trail runs along Abrams Creek the entire journey to the falls. This MODERATELY DIFFICULT trail is a very popular family hike.

HOW LONG IS THIS HIKE? This Scavenger Hike Adventure is 5 miles round-trip. You should allow 3 to 4 hours.

SPECIAL COMMENT: Cades Cove has a one-way 11-mile road that loops around the valley. The Abrams Falls trailhead is located about halfway around the big loop. Before you head out on the loop, you might want to stop at the campground store to get a sandwich or an ice-cream cone! Traffic on the loop often comes to a standstill when a visitor sees a bear. Locals call that a "bear jam." You won't be able to hurry around the loop. Oh, by the way, have we mentioned that this road is a loop? Remember, though, *the journey is the destination.*

THINGS TO HUNT FOR

(Earn 10 points for each treasure you find.)

1

FIND A DEER!

(As you enter the Cades Cove Loop—
go on to #2 as you search.)

SPECIAL HINT: You have 5 miles to spot a deer
before you get to the Abrams Falls trailhead.
Ready . . . Set . . . Go!!!

10 POINTS

2

FIND A BLACK BEAR!

(As you drive along the Cades Cove Loop—
go on to #3 as you search.)

SPECIAL HINT: After you find a deer, search for a black bear!
Don't forget to look up in trees and deep into the woods. There
are about 1,500 bears in this park. A black bear weighs
less than a can of soda at birth and can
grow to more than 400 pounds. Try
to find just one.

*Never approach
a bear. Keep
your distance!*

10 POINTS

3
FIND A WILD TURKEY!
(On the way to the trailhead)

SPECIAL HINT: While you're searching for a bear and a deer, you might as well keep your eye out for the biggest bird in the park. In the spring, male wild turkeys can be heard gobbling from a mile away. Roll your window down!

10 POINTS

4
FIND THE SITE of John Oliver's Guest Lodge!
(Just before reaching the footbridge at the trailhead)

SPECIAL HINT: Look for the large grouping of hemlock trees (short needles about as long as your fingernail). Gently rub the needles of the tree between your thumb and fingers, and then take a whiff. Now, the next time someone asks if you have ever really smelled a hemlock tree say, **"Uh"** (Cherokee for "yes"), and then say, **"Zee-yookt guh-noh-hee-ahay"** (Cherokee for "I speak the truth"). Cherokee Indians lived in the Cades Cove area, and Abrams Falls is named for **Cherokee Chief Abram.** By the way, John Oliver's guest lodge stood right here about 80 years ago. He was the great-grandson of the first white settler, also named John Oliver, who came to Cades Cove in the fall of 1818.

◯

10 POINTS

5

FIND THE "THERMOMETER" JUNGLE!
(After you cross the footbridge)

SPECIAL HINT: Search for an evergreen plant with very long, narrow and thick leaves. Its flowers bloom in the summer. Pioneers used these leaves as "thermometers." When the leaves darken and droop, it is about 32 degrees. At around 20 degrees the leaves curl and roll up. At 0 degrees, the leaves roll up as tight as a pencil. How cool is that? By the way, the Cherokee would put a leaf on their forehead to heal a headache. They didn't have Advil back then. ***Remember, never ever pick a leaf or damage any plant life. Each plant is protected by our national park!***

◯

10 POINTS

6

FIND A SIGN OF A BEAR!
(Search all along the trail to the falls—go
on to #7 as you keep your eyes wide open.)

SPECIAL HINT: Look for dead logs and trees that were clawed open or shredded by bears looking for grubs and other critter snacks. There are a lot of signs of bears along this trail.

Hmmmmm! When cold weather is just around the corner, bears in the Smokies often find a hollow tree high above the ground to sleep in for the winter. Look up!

10 POINTS

7

FIND A LIVING CREATURE in the Stream!

(Between here and the falls, stop by the stream and take a close look.)

SPECIAL HINT: Years ago river otters were abundant here. In fact, the Cherokee Indians once called this area, **"Tsiyahai,"** meaning "place of the otter." The otters were trapped for their fur and became extinct in the park. In 1986 the park reintroduced river otters into the Abrams Creek area. Who knows? Maybe you'll find a river otter, a fish, a water strider (looks like a floating spider with only six legs), a salamander, or a snake!

10 POINTS

8

FIND THE GARGANTUAN (GIANT) WHITE PINE TREE!

(Walk quite a ways—this tree is on the left edge of the trail)

SPECIAL HINT: You'll walk quite a ways before you find this giant of the forest. You will pass several large trees, but when you reach this tree you will say, "That has got to be it!" It has thick reddish brown bark with deep furrows, and *two normal-*

PROTECT THE GREAT SMOKY MOUNTAINS NATIONAL PARK

size pioneers arm to arm could not encircle this tree trunk! Key hint: It is located just **on the edge** of the trail. To be sure you found the right tree, find a deep hole at the base of this giant tree trunk. Also, the long needles come in bunches of five.

10 POINTS

9

FIND THE GALAX! (Pronounced *GAY-lax*)

(92 steps past the giant white pine. Look on the right side of the trail—on the side of the hill.)

SPECIAL HINT: This is a very *shiny* evergreen plant that grows low to the ground. Its leaves are kind of circular, or perhaps like a fat heart shape. Galax grows only in the Southern Appalachian Mountains. It blooms a pillar of tiny white flowers in late spring and early summer, and they smell like *garlic*. Mountain people used to gather galax, which turns crimson in the fall, and sell it to florists who used it in bouquets and other floral arrangements. ***Remember, never pick anything or take anything from the park!***

10 POINTS

10

FIND THE NATURAL ROCK SEAT AND STAIRWAY!

(At the top of the hill)

SPECIAL HINT: When you reach the top of the ridge, look to your right for a tree that grew right through a rock. There are so many rocks and such little soil that this tree's roots are searching every which way for food and water. The rock seat is right below that tree, and the stairway (rocks) leads down the hill at that point. In the spring the seat is totally surrounded by a bouquet of beautiful **mountain laurel**. Definitely a photo op!

10 POINTS

11

FIND THE LAUREL HELL!

(Located just before the log footbridge)

SPECIAL HINT: The pioneers called this tangled quagmire of rhododendron bushes a "laurel hell" because it was very hard to walk through. Back then rhododendron was called "laurel." Imagine you and your family trying to get to Aunt Lucinda's cabin through this thicket!

10 POINTS

12

FIND THE WHITE-WATER CASCADE!

(Count 70 steps after you cross the log footbridge.)

SPECIAL HINT: Look in the creek at the water flowing over the rocks. This is called a **cascade.** Hope you have at least one more shot left in your camera!

10 POINTS

13

FIND THE YELLOW LICHEN on the Rocks!

(You will hike for quite a while. Located near the top of the next hill—on the right on the rocks)

SPECIAL HINT: The trail is level for quite a ways before you reach the next steep hill. This lichen (pronounced *LIKE-in*) is growing on the rocks and looks like bright-yellow spray paint! Lichen is a combination of **algae and fungus.** The acid in lichen gradually eats away at the rock, breaking it into very tiny particles that eventually become soil. If you come to the hairpin curve that goes to the right, you are 40 steps *past* the lichen!!!

10 POINTS

14
FIND THE DOG-HOBBLE!
(Located about 12 steps from the middle
point of the giant U-turn on the right)

SPECIAL HINT: As you go down the long steep hill, you will see the perfect U-turn in the trail down below. The only way to tell for sure if you have found the dog-hobble is to run your finger back and forth along the edge of a leaf. If you can feel the jagged edges, you have found it! Dogs would get stuck, or hobbled, in these bushes as they chased after bears. That's why the mountain folks called it dog-hobble. Dog-hobble only grows in the Southern Appalachian Mountains. This means that dogs in Chicago and other major metropolitan regions don't have to worry about it!

10 POINTS

15

FIND THE TREE with a Bad "Root" Day!

(Cross a log footbridge. Walk quite
awhile—go up a long hill.)

SPECIAL HINT: You'll see many roots along the way, but these are the only roots that form a **"rooty" seat.** Need a break? Sit on a root! You actually have to walk around these wacky tree roots to stay on the trail! Have you ever had a bad "hair" day? Well, it looks like this tree is having a bad "root" day!

10 POINTS

16

FIND THE WARNING SIGN!

(On the left—at the top of the hill)

SPECIAL HINT: Abrams Falls is a powerful waterfall and one of the slipperiest areas in the park. This warning sign is here for a reason. *Be extremely careful around the falls!*

10 POINTS

17

FIND THE SMOOTHEST HYPNOTIC CASCADE
You've Ever Seen!

(Just before you reach the next log
footbridge—before the falls)

SPECIAL HINT: The water just seems to magi-
cally glide over the rocks. This cascade is almost
hypnotic in beauty!

10 POINTS

18

FIND ABRAMS FALLS and
the Awesome Deep Pool!

(You made it!)

SPECIAL HINT: Relax, take a break, have a snack, take a nap,
read a book, take a look. You must be beat; dan-
gle your feet, take a sip, eat a chip! Enjoy it. You
deserve it!

10 POINTS

19

FIND ELIJAH OLIVER'S CABIN!

(Look for a sign before you reach the footbridge
near the start of the trail.)

SPECIAL HINT: You can find Elijah Oliver's cabin, smokehouse, stable, springhouse, corncrib, barn, and small cabin
guest room by walking a half mile down the side trail. Too

tired? Then check out his cabin on the cover of *Scavenger Hike Adventures!* Elijah was the son of the first white settler in Cades Cove, John Oliver. What's cool about this cabin is the little room that he built right on the front porch. It was used for guests and was called the "stranger room." Give yourself 20 points if you hike to the actual cabin or 10 points if you just find it on the cover of this book!

10 POINTS

PROTECT THE GREAT SMOKY MOUNTAINS NATIONAL PARK

CONGRATULATIONS!

You have just completed a

Great Smoky Mountains National Park

Scavenger Hike Adventure!

Cades Cove to Abrams Falls Trail to Abrams Falls

10 points for each item found

Total Score _____

Certified Achievement Level _____

50 to 100 points: *City Slicker*

Over **100 to 140** points: *Pioneer Scout*

Over **140** points: *Frontier Explorer*

Name(s): _____

_____

Witness(es) thereof: _____

Date: _____

Journal Notes

The people on this hike were:

_____

_____

_____

The weather was:

_____

_____

_____

We saw:

_____

_____

_____

_____

More about our adventure:

_____

_____

_____

_____

_____

Scavenger Hike Adventure

9

Fighting Creek Nature Trail

WHY THIS IS A GREAT TRAIL! On this Scavenger Hike Adventure we guarantee that you will see a black bear, a wild turkey, a red-cheeked salamander (that lives only in the Smokies and nowhere else on earth!), a white-tailed deer, and a wild hog! You will walk a mile in the moccasins of Cherokee Indians, who hunted and maybe even farmed in this area! In the middle 1800s a community of settlers lived here. This community was called "Forks of the River." Back then there were about 25 farmsteads in Forks of the River! You will find the authentic log cabin of pioneer John Ownby and his old-time "refrigerator"! You will find the strangest sycamore tree that you will ever see in your lifetime! If that's not enough, you'll find a cornfield that a pioneer almost fell out of!

WHERE'S THE TRAIL? From the Sugarlands Visitor Center, simply follow the path that leads behind the building and you will see a sign for FIGHTING CREEK NATURE TRAIL.

ABOUT THE TRAIL: This EASY Scavenger Hike Adventure is on a trail that is a bit hilly, but even an inexperienced small pioneer can handle it! There are also benches along the way for taking an occasional break. The trail is wide enough for two pioneers to walk side by side. You'll walk alongside and across Fighting Creek!

HOW LONG IS THIS HIKE? This Scavenger Hike Adventure is a bit less than a mile round-trip and will take about an hour to complete. It starts behind the Sugarlands Visitor Center and loops back to the same point.

THINGS TO HUNT FOR

(Earn 10 points for each treasure you find.)

1

FIND A BLACK BEAR, a Wild Turkey, a White-Tailed Deer, a Wild Hog, and a Red-Cheeked Salamander (Found Only in the Smokies and Nowhere Else on Earth)!

(You might find *some* of these animals along the trail, but . . .)

SPECIAL HINT: You'll be *sure* to find them in the Sugarlands Visitor Center! It's a great place. Don't miss it!

10 POINTS

2

FIND THE CORNFIELDS That Pioneers Planted That Aren't There Anymore!

(Near Marker #2—look to the left and right.)

SPECIAL HINT: You are standing in the middle of what was once a pioneer's cornfield! Whenever you see a group of tall skinny trees (tulip trees), you are very likely looking at what was once a farm field. Across from Marker #2 there is a very tall tulip tree. Look up high to find the leaf, which is shaped kind of like a tulip flower. Sometimes you need binoculars to see the leaves on these very tall trees! Mountain folks liked to use this tall, straight tree for building cabins and barns. The tulip trees grew so big, pioneers could build an entire cabin out of one tree!

10 POINTS

3
FIND THE FURRY VINE!
(Near Marker #2)

SPECIAL HINT: This poison ivy is climbing a tree, and even though it looks like it is covered with fur, *do not pet it!* Why not? You would itch like crazy! Poison ivy also grows on the ground and can be identified by its groupings of three leaves. Two good rhymes to remember are "Leaves of three, let it be!" and "Furry vine, itch in time!" Poison ivy's grapelike clusters of fruits are a favorite of many birds in the Smokies! Even though the fruit also contains the "poison," it doesn't bother the birds one bit! Lucky birds!

10 POINTS

4
FIND THE OLD ROAD That Pioneer Kids Used to Walk to School!
(At Marker #3—look toward the creek.)

SPECIAL HINT: There are three roads at this spot in the trail.
Road #1—The actual creekbed was the first "road" that Indians and pioneers used. That was a very rough and wet road!
Road #2—The settlers cleared roads right *next* to the creek.
Road #3—Then mountain folks built roads on higher levels to avoid flood situations. The trail you are hiking on is Road #3.
Can you find Road #2?

Pioneer children walked on Road #2 all the way to **Fighting Creek School,** about a half mile downstream! Pioneer families also walked to church down this road! People lived in Forks of the River until 1935, when they had to leave because it was decided the Smoky Mountains would become a national park!

○ **10 POINTS**

5
FIND THE STRANGELY SHAPED ROCKING CHAIR TREE!
(Just before you cross the footbridge)

SPECIAL HINT: Old-timers say a pioneer used the wood from this tree to build rocking chairs, and as he kept pruning the tree branches to make the chairs, it grew in a very wild and crazy way! Sycamore trees were also used by pioneers to make butcher blocks. By the way, this is a sycamore tree! You will now cross **Fighting Creek.** Are you wondering how it got its name? One reason is that the folks here fought a lot about where the community's school would be built. So they ended up calling the creek in the area Fighting Creek and the school Fighting Creek School!

○ **10 POINTS**

6
FIND THE DOG TRAP!
(18 steps after you cross the footbridge—on the left)

SPECIAL HINT: Look for the evergreen plant that has sharp edges on its leathery leaves. It grows low to the ground, and in the pioneer days dogs would get trapped, or "hobbled," in the tangled growth. That's why this shrub was called dog-hobble by the pioneers! To really be sure you have found the dog-hobble, run your finger along the edge of a leaf. Does it feel sharp? Yes! You found the dog-hobble! ***Remember! Protect every treasure in the Great Smoky Mountains National Park! Don't pick anything! Don't take anything! Don't leave anything!***

10 POINTS

7
FIND THE *WILD*, WILD GRAPEVINES!
(68 steps past the dog-hobble you just found—look around.)

SPECIAL HINT: The woody vines are growing around the tree, up the tree, and down the tree! You can find lots of wild grapevines in the Smoky Mountains! Opossums and many other Smoky Mountain critters eat the sour wild grapes! Cherokee Indians would burn grapevines with oak because they believed it would bring a spell of warm weather in the middle of a cold winter. Cherokee Indians lived here long, long ago and still live on the Qualla Indian Reservation on the other side of the mountains in Cherokee, North Carolina.

10 POINTS

8

FIND WHERE PIONEER Noah McCarter lived!

(Near Marker #5)

SPECIAL HINT: Find the dark-green round-shaped bush with tiny oval leaves. This is a **boxwood.** Also find yucca plants that are low to the ground with leaves that are long, narrow, and pointed. These plants were used to landscape around the homestead. They are not native to the Smokies!
Any time you see landscaping plants like these or yellow daffodils, a pioneer likely lived nearby.

10 POINTS

9

FIND THE FAMILY GARDEN!

(Stand at the boxwood bush and face north.)

SPECIAL HINT: Use the sun to find the direction and look across the trail. This pioneer family's garden was to the right of the cabin location. Settlers grew most of their own food. To feel like a pioneer, stop right where you are and pretend that you are going to build a cabin, farm this land, and provide for your family starting right here . . .
today! You have a lot of hard work ahead of you! Early settlers had a tough row to hoe!

10 POINTS

10

FIND THE TREE in the Middle of the Trail!

(Between Markers #5 and #6)

SPECIAL HINT: You are searching for a maple tree growing smack-dab in the middle of the trail. Just don't run into it and bang your head!

10 POINTS

11

FIND THE CHRISTMAS FERNS!

(Go 10 steps from the tree that you just found— look on the right.)

SPECIAL HINT: Some folks say that each individual fern leaf is shaped like Santa's sleigh; others say it is shaped like a Christmas stocking! Look to your right as you go up the hillside to find a Christmas fern. In the summer they may be hidden a bit, but as Southerners might say, "Mayon— naise—a lot of 'em up there on the hill!" *Remember! Never pick anything, never take anything, and protect each and every plant and animal in this park!*

10 POINTS

12

FIND THE TREE That Once Blocked the Trail!

(Right before Marker #7—near the top of the hill)

SPECIAL HINT: The space between the rings in the trunk of the tree will be narrow for a very dry year and a bit wider for a very rainy year. **Each ring is one-year's growth.** If you are tired, lie on the bench, close your eyes, and count tree rings!

10 POINTS

13

FIND THE LARGE ROCK Where an "X" Marks the Spot!

(Immediately after you cross the next footbridge)

SPECIAL HINT: This rock has two cracks in it shaped very much like an X. When water on a rock freezes, it expands in the little crevices and cracks the rock. That could be what happened to this one!

10 POINTS

14

FIND THE WOODEN PEGS on the Cabin!

(On only one of the outside four corners of John Ownby's cabin)

SPECIAL HINT: Find the top of the wooden pegs used to hold the cabin together. Mysteriously, they are found only on one outside corner of this cabin!

10 POINTS

15

FIND JOHN OWNBY'S "REFRIGERATOR"!

(Go through the cabin and head toward the hill—look for the stream and a stack of rocks.)

SPECIAL HINT: John Ownby built a small shed around the spring, and the flowing water kept his eggs and milk cool. A **springhouse** was a pioneer's refrigerator. How cool is that?

10 POINTS

16

FIND THE CORNFIELD a Pioneer Could Have Fallen Out Of!

(As you leave the spring, take 10 steps toward the cabin.)

Special Hint: Look up to your left. Corn was actually grown on this steep hill. Mountain people joked about "falling out of their cornfields"! At harvest time, pioneers used sleds to take the corn out of these steep fields!

10 POINTS

17
FIND SOMETHING You Really Need Bad!
(Cross the footbridge and go to Marker #10.)

SPECIAL HINT: This is a long hill! You may need a _ _ _ _ _!
Some folks think Smoky Mountain benches are
another Smoky Mountain **treasure,** especially
when they are tired and need a break!   **10 POINTS**

18
FIND THE "WINDOW" through the Old Oak Tree!
(From Marker #10 take one sharp right turn, then before the
next sharp right turn—stop and look.)

SPECIAL HINT: Before heading down the hill, look to the right
of the path for a tree trunk that splits into a Y and creates a
"window" down into the valley. There is **a rock**
at the base of this tree that a shorter person may
use as a footstool to peer through the "window"
of this tree!   **10 POINTS**

19

FIND THE AMAZING WALL OF ROOTS!

(You'll hike awhile. Look at the bottom of the hill—
as the trail bends to the left.)

SPECIAL HINT: Two trees were blown over to create this incredible wall of roots! These trees will most likely become a home for many plants and animals in this forest! Check it out! Do you see any plants or Smoky Mountain critters that have decided to make it "home sweet home"? Don't forget to stop by the Sugarlands Visitor Center and take a good look at all the critters that live in our national park! You can also watch a *great* 20-minute movie all about the Smoky Mountains!

10 POINTS

CONGRATULATIONS!

You have just completed a

Great Smoky Mountains National Park

Scavenger Hike Adventure!

Fighting Creek Nature Trail

10 points for each item found

Total Score _____

Certified Achievement Level _____

50 to 100 points: *City Slicker*

Over **100 to 170** points: *Pioneer Scout*

Over **170** points: *Frontier Explorer*

Name(s): _____

_____

Witness(es) thereof: _____

Date: _____

Journal Notes

The people on this hike were:

_____

_____

_____

The weather was:

_____

_____

_____

We saw:

_____

_____

_____

More about our adventure:

_____

_____

_____

_____

_____

Scavenger Hike Adventure

Smokemont Nature Trail

WHY THIS IS A GREAT TRAIL! Camping in Smokemont near Cherokee, North Carolina? This trail is just a short walk from your pup tent! Don't miss this pleasant mountain Scavenger Hike Adventure on the North Carolina side of the Smokies! This is a narrow, sometimes rather steep trail that is **very do-able for families.** The trail loops around a mountain ridge through a former logging area! You'll find three log footbridges that total more than 100 feet long crossing over the beautiful mountain stream. You'll search for one of the most unusual chestnut tree hulks imaginable. It is HUGE! You'll hike through a rhododendron and mountain laurel "jungle." You will loop up, around, and back down the mountain. You'll

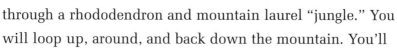

definitely be comin' roun' the mountain when you come! Excellent for pioneers of all ages.

WHERE'S THE TRAIL? This trail is located 3 miles north of the Oconaluftee Visitor Center near the Cherokee, North Carolina, entrance to the park. From the Sugarlands Visitor Center, you should head straight over the mountains toward Cherokee on Newfound Gap Road (U.S. Highway 441). Enter the Smokemont campground and drive to Section B, where there is parking at the trailhead.

ABOUT THE TRAIL: Smokemont Nature Trail is rather narrow, sometimes a bit steep, but pretty EASY.

HOW LONG IS THIS HIKE? This trail is about a ¾-mile loop and will take less than an hour.

THINGS TO HUNT FOR
(Earn 10 points for each treasure you find.)

1
FIND THE TRIPLE FOOTBRIDGE!
(Located at the trailhead—cross only the first two bridges, and then stop and find Item #2.)

SPECIAL HINT: You'll cross mountain streams on **three footbridges** that, in total, span more than 100 feet! This is an awe-

some stream! It is beautiful Bradley Fork!
(Remember, don't cross the third log bridge
until you complete Clue #2.) ◯

10 POINTS

2
FIND THE "THERMOMETER" BUSHES!
(Look around between the second and third footbridges.)

SPECIAL HINT: Find the bush that has long, narrow evergreen leaves that feel almost like leather. These are rhododendron bushes! The pioneers knew that at 32 degrees, the leaves darken and droop; at 20 degrees they begin to curl up; and at 0 degrees the leaves curl up as tight as pencils! It is a "thermometer" in the woods! These rhododendron bushes bloom in early summer! ◯

10 POINTS

3
FIND THE "LANDING ZONE"
for Smoky Mountain Northern Flying Squirrels!
(After you cross the third log footbridge—go 10 steps, curving right on a small path leading down to the stream.)

SPECIAL HINT: Look at the boulder next to the stream. Do you see something that looks like brownish-colored crumpled leaves growing on the rocks? This is rock tripe, a favorite snack of **northern flying squirrels!** It is a lichen (pronounced *LIKE-in*), a combination of fungus and algae. This rock tripe releases an acid that eats away at the rock. This acid will eventually break this rock into fine particles that will eventually become soil. Pretty amazing, huh? Don't eat the rock tripe unless you are a flying squirrel! Northern flying squirrels are generally found in higher elevations in the park, so they may find a different landing zone to enjoy this snack!

◯ **10 POINTS**

4

FIND THE SPOON, I MEAN "FORK"
in the River!

(As you hike up the ridge of the mountain—
look down at the stream.)

SPECIAL HINT: Find where the beautiful stream splits like a **kitchen fork with two prongs!**

◯ **10 POINTS**

5

FIND THE LOGGING VILLAGE Down Below!

(At Marker #2, look down into the valley—on the right.)

SPECIAL HINT: It is hard to believe that this campground area below you once had homes, a store, and a railroad and was a bustling logging community! Before this area was a park, a logging company cut down most of the trees, including those on the mountain you are now climbing! That is why the forest all around you is called a **second-growth forest!**

◯ **10 POINTS**

6

FIND THE BENCH and Take a "Smell" Break!

(Near Marker #4)

SPECIAL HINT: The evergreen tree behind the log has short, flat needles with two white stripes on the underside of each needle. If you gently rub the needles between your fingers, they give off a great smell! Take a smell break! This tree is a hemlock. Now you know how to identify one of the more than 130 different kinds (species) of trees in the Great Smoky Mountains National Park!

10 POINTS

7

FIND THE HILL OF ROOTS!

(Located near Marker #6)

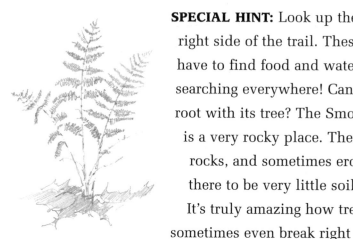

SPECIAL HINT: Look up the hill on the right side of the trail. These tree roots have to find food and water! They are searching everywhere! Can you match a root with its tree? The Smoky Mountains is a very rocky place. There are lots of rocks, and sometimes erosion causes there to be very little soil on the trail! It's truly amazing how tree roots will sometimes even break right through rocks in the Smokies looking for food and water!

10 POINTS

8

FIND THE MOUNTAIN LAUREL JUNGLE!

(45 steps past Marker #6)

SPECIAL HINT: You are surrounded by **mountain laurel!**
Mountain laurel looks a lot like rhododendron but has narrower
and shorter evergreen leaves. Mountain laurel has beautiful
white and pink flowers that bloom in the spring and summer in
higher elevations. Pioneers called it "ivy." Cherokee Indians
who lived in the Smokies long long ago and still live in
Cherokee, North Carolina, today called mountain laurel **spoon-
wood** because they carved spoons from it! If
you're lucky, you'll be hiking in a beautiful bouquet of flowers!

10 POINTS

9

FIND THE TREE That Blew Over
and Landed on the Trail!

(Go 20 steps past Marker #8.)

SPECIAL HINT: Park rangers had to cut this tree with a chain saw to make an opening for you to get through! Special thanks to our park rangers who help take care of this beautiful park! *It is up to all of us to protect every single treasure in the Smoky Mountains! Remember! Don't take anything! Don't pick anything! And don't leave anything!*

○

10 POINTS

10

FIND A CHRISTMAS FERN!

(At Marker #10)

SPECIAL HINT: Some folks think that the individual leaves of this fern are shaped like Santa's sleigh or a Christmas stocking. That is why it was named Christmas Fern! What do you think? There are many very beautiful ferns in the Smoky Mountains!

○

10 POINTS

11
FIND THE GRAY GHOST!
(24 steps past Marker #11)

SPECIAL HINT: Look up the hill—on the left. This is the remains of a giant **American chestnut tree.** Wow! In the early 1900s these trees were wiped out by a blight (disease). The mountain folks thought the huge gray stumps looked like gray ghosts in the evening mist. It was said that cabins built from a chestnut tree would never rot! Bears loved the chestnuts, and so did people! Bears are smaller today than they were when they had chestnuts **10 POINTS** to eat!

SPECIAL COMMENTS: Visit the campground office and check out the display of old photographs taken during the logging days! Smokemont sure didn't look like a campground back then!

On your way out of the campground, park right before the bridge and walk up the hill to the **Lufty Baptist Church,** established in 1836. Go inside and take a look at where early settlers worshipped!

CONGRATULATIONS!

You have just completed a

Great Smoky Mountains National Park

Scavenger Hike Adventure!

Smokemont Nature Trail

10 points for each item found

Total Score _____

Certified Achievement Level _____

50 to 70 points: *City Slicker*

Over **70 to 90** points: *Pioneer Scout*

Over **90** points: *Frontier Explorer*

Name(s): _____

_____

Witness(es) thereof: _____

_____

Date:_____

Journal Notes

The people on this hike were:

_____

_____

_____

_____

The weather was:

_____

_____

_____

_____

We saw:

_____

_____

_____

_____

More about our adventure:

_____

_____

_____

_____

_____

Scavenger Hike Adventure

Grapeyard Ridge Trail to
Steam Engine Wreck

WHY THIS IS A GREAT TRAIL! This Scavenger Hike
Adventure will lead you through Rhododendron Valley, one
of the most peaceful and beautiful narrow lowland valleys
imaginable! You will find the area where Dolly Parton's grand-
father, Walter Parton, once lived. You will cross streams a challenging half dozen times. There are no footbridges, and one
stream is almost 10 feet wide! You won't believe it when you
find a steam engine that rolled off the side of the mountain and
landed in Injun Creek! Depending on the time of year, you
might not even see one other hiker on this beautiful trail in the
quieter and less busy Greenbrier section of the park!

WHERE'S THE TRAIL? From the Sugarlands Visitor Center go
north on U.S. Highway 441 into Gatlinburg. Be sure to merge
into the right lane when you see the Hard Rock Cafe, and then

veer right onto U.S. Highway 321 at **Stoplight #3.** Stoplights in Gatlinburg are all numbered. Follow US 321 approximately 6 miles to the Greenbrier entrance of the Great Smoky Mountains National Park. Turn right into the park and drive along the Little Pigeon River on Greenbrier Road for about 3 miles until you see the bridge and road that leads to Ramsey Cascades Trail. Park on the left side of Greenbrier Road before the bridge. The trailhead is on the right side of the road.

ABOUT THE TRAIL: This EXTREME trail climbs a ridge before it heads down into Rhododendron Valley. After about 2 miles, the trail heads uphill for $\frac{7}{10}$ mile to the top of James Gap. Then it heads downhill for $\frac{2}{10}$ mile to the steam engine wreck lying in Injun Creek. It is a fairly solid uphill trek to the top of James Gap.

HOW LONG IS THIS HIKE? This Scavenger Hike Adventure is a little over 6 miles round-trip. It is do-able in 3 to 4 hours.

THINGS TO HUNT FOR

(Earn 10 points for each treasure you find.)

1

FIND THE ANSWERS to Two Smoky Mountain Fishing Questions!

(Across the road from the trailhead)

SPECIAL HINT: Answer true or false.

1. It is a good idea to use worms and corn for bait when fishing in the park. (T or F)
2. The maximum number of fish you can keep is two per day. (T or F)

10 POINTS

2

FIND THE PICTURE WINDOW!

(Just as you start up the trail—look to the left.)

SPECIAL HINT: Look for two trees bordering a large rock. The trees and the rock form a perfect **"picture window"** overlooking a beautiful view of the cascading creek across Greenbrier Road! Two creeks, the Middle Prong of the Little Pigeon River and Porter's Creek, come tumbling out of the mountains and join together here to become the Little Pigeon River! *Warning: Don't touch the furry vine growing around the "frame" of the picture window—POISON IVY!*

10 POINTS

3

FIND THE ROCK WALL Built by the Young Men of the CCC!

(As you continue a few steps up the ridge—look to the right.)

SPECIAL HINT: The Civilian Conservation Corps had a camp near the trailhead just east of Greenbrier Road. The CCC was a program started by the U.S. government in the 1930s to give jobs to young men during the Depression when few jobs were available. Those young men of the CCC built this rock wall and built this *entire trail.* We can thank the CCC for many of the trails and bridges in the park! If you need to mail something or get some groceries, there is a grocery store and post office right below the rock wall. Oh, sorry, I guess that was about 80 years ago! The only thing left now above the wall is a piece of a chimney from Friendship Church.

10 POINTS

4

FIND THE WOOD That the Cherokee Indians Believed Would Change the Weather!

(Between here and the steam engine wreck)

SPECIAL HINT: Find a wild grapevine! Cherokee Indians have lived in the Smokies for about 1,000 years. They believed that burning the wood of a grapevine with oak would bring a warm spell of weather in the middle of a cold winter. If it looks like a grapevine but has a furry cover, you've probably found poison ivy! KEEP LOOKING! This entire area was once called **Winnesoka,** Cherokee for "Place of the Grapes." White settlers did not use that name but did use the name "grapeyard" for the high ridge extending above Round Top Mountain. When this trail was built, it was also named Grapeyard Ridge, linking back to the original Cherokee name Winnesoka!

10 POINTS

5

FIND A SPECIAL PLANT That Is Only Found in the Appalachian Mountains!

(Search all along the trail up this ridge.)

SPECIAL HINT: Find galax (pronounced *GAY-lax*), a plant with very shiny green leaves shaped like fat hearts. It grows only a few inches off the ground. In the spring and summer it blooms a white pillar of flowers that smell like garlic. The mountain folks would sell the galax leaves to florists for use in floral arrangements. In the fall, galax turns crimson. If you can't find them here, you can always search in Galax, Virginia!

Remember: Don't pick anything! All plants are protected by our national park. Picking a plant or flower can bring a stiff fine from the federal government.

10 POINTS

6

FIND THE REMAINS of a Settler's Homesite!

(Hike about 10 to 15 minutes. Look on the right at eye level
—at the top of the hill where the trail sharply bends to the
right and starts heading down.)

SPECIAL HINT: Look for the mound of rocks that was once the
chimney and fireplace about 30 feet to the right of the trail.
This pioneer had a choice corner lot on top of this beautiful
ridge! *Remember: It is about a 15-minute hike from the start
of the trail to the top of this first hill.* There is a
very large curving bend to the right as it heads
down into Rhododendron Valley.   **10 POINTS**

7

FIND A STAND OF HEMLOCK TREES!

(On the left—as you head down the hill
from the settlers' homesite)

SPECIAL HINT: A grouping of the same kind of tree is called a
"stand." Find the stand of hemlocks. A hemlock needle is
about as long as a fingernail and has two faint white stripes on
the underside. Hemlocks in the park are
being attacked by an insect called
the hemlock woolly adelgid (*a-
DELL-jid*). Hemlocks cool the
mountain streams; if they
die, the water temperature
will rise and then threaten fish

and other animals. Seven species of songbirds depend on hem-locks for food and shelter. In nature it seems everything is connected. Rangers are doing everything they can to save these important trees.

◯

10 POINTS

8

FIND A SIGN OF A BEAR!

(Look all along the trail from here to the wrecked engine—go on to #9 as you keep your eyes wide open.)

SPECIAL HINT: This is a fairly secluded trail, and there are about two bears for every square mile in the park! Remember you drove more than 3 miles deep into the woods on Greenbrier Road before you even started this hike! Look for a tree or log that was clawed open by a bear searching for insects to eat. Bears also eat berries and yellow jackets! Look for black bear scat—which is often a shiny blackish blue when berries are in season. There is a lot of bear activity on this trail! Keep your eyes wide open! If you can't find any sign of a bear, *but actually find a bear along the trail—go ahead and give yourself the points anyway!*

◯

10 POINTS

9

FIND THE SITE of Avery Whaley's
Farm and Orchard!

(After you cross the first stream, look on the left and right of
the trail for flat, open areas.)

SPECIAL HINT: The skinny trees and open spaces around you
are a clue that this was once a cleared farm field. Avery Whaley
had about 50 apple trees in his orchard, and he also farmed
this area. Many families once lived along the rich "bottom-
land" near the creek in this beautiful valley! You
may notice the "zillions" of delicate **ladyferns**
all along the trail!

10 POINTS

10

FIND THE AREA ONCE HOME TO WALTER
PARTON, Dolly Parton's Grandfather!

(Just before you cross the second stream, find the
remains of a rock wall on the left.)

SPECIAL HINT: This area certainly wasn't
Dolly's Woods, but it was Walter's Woods!
Many of Dolly's kinfolk lived in what is now the
national park. Walter Parton lived up above the
creek in this area on the left. He
definitely didn't work just 9
to 5!

10 POINTS

11

FIND THE QUARTZ BOULDERS!

(40 steps past the second stream crossing)

SPECIAL HINT: Look for a whitish-brownish-orange boulder the size of a wheelbarrow! It should be easy to spot. There are a few of them along the trail here.

10 POINTS

12

FIND RHODODENDRON VALLEY!

(All around you as you continue past the quartz boulders)

SPECIAL HINT: The rhododendron bush has long, narrow evergreen leaves that feel almost like leather. Mountain folks used to call rhododendron "laurel," so this valley was originally called Laurel Valley. When the park was formed, there were too many Laurel Creeks and Laurel Valleys, so they changed the name of this creek and the valley to **Rhododendron.** There are also many mountain laurel bushes in this valley. They look similar to rhododendron bushes, except the leaves are smaller. When mountain laurel or rhododendron is in bloom, you may feel like you are walking through a postcard!

10 POINTS

13

FIND THE LOG ACROSS THE CREEK That Could Lead You in the Wrong Direction!

(At the next stream crossing)

SPECIAL HINT: You'll come to a very wide stream crossing. There is a tree that fell across the stream on the left, and it is a tempting bridge! ***Caution: This log points away from the actual trail and is a hazardous route!*** The trail picks up a bit upstream from the crossing point (to your right). Your best bet is to use the rocks as stepping-stones, or give it up and just wade through the shallow stream. ***Veer to the right immediately after you cross the stream*** to get back on the trail!

10 POINTS

14

FIND THE FENCE POSTS!

(Cross three more streams—search on the right side of the trail.)

SPECIAL HINT: Some of the fence posts still have barbed wire attached! If you are really observant, you can determine the entire area that this settler fenced in. Another clue is to look carefully about 20 steps before you reach a small low-lying water crossing. Good luck. This one is kind of tough!

10 POINTS

15
FIND SIGNS OF WILD HOGS!

(Along the trail—between here and the steam engine wreck.
Go on to #16 while you search.)

SPECIAL HINT: Look for areas on the ground and even on the side of the trail where wild hogs used their snouts and root the ground to find food. The wild hogs eat about anything on the ground, including snails, snakes, acorns, roots, flowers, and salamanders. Some park rangers are employed full-time to hunt for hogs because they are not native to the park, and they destroy plant life and pollute the streams. Hundreds still roam the park at night!   **10 POINTS**

16
FIND THE CABIN LOCATION at the
Absolute Top of James Gap!

(After you finally make it to the top of the ridge—about ⁷/₁₀ mile uphill hike—find the mound of rocks above you on the right marking the fireplace and location of the cabin.)

SPECIAL HINT: It is a long, challenging hike up to this gap! You may wonder if you will ever make it. You will! The steam engine wreck is only ²/₁₀ of a mile down from here. *Remember, the return hike is mainly downhill!*   **10 POINTS**

17

FIND THE STEAM ENGINE WRECK!

(Head down the hill—look in the creek.)

SPECIAL HINT: This old steam engine was self-propelled and was used for logging. It rolled off the mountain more than 80 years ago. The steam engine was being used to help build a school. It's been said that the engineer jumped to safety and did not get hurt.

10 POINTS

18

FIND THE NAME OF THE COMPANY
That Manufactured This Steam Engine!

(Located on the engine)

SPECIAL HINT: Head down toward the engine! This is a very unique historical treasure of the Smokies!

10 POINTS

CONGRATULATIONS!

You have just completed a

Great Smoky Mountains National Park

Scavenger Hike Adventure!

Grapeyard Ridge Trail to Steam Engine Wreck

10 points for each item found

Total Score _____

Certified Achievement Level _____

50 to 100 points: *City Slicker*

Over **100 to 150** points: *Pioneer Scout*

Over **150** points: *Frontier Explorer*

Name(s): _____

_____

Witness(es) thereof: _____

Date: _____

Journal Notes

The people on this hike were:

_____

_____

_____

The weather was:

_____

_____

_____

We saw:

_____

_____

_____

More about our adventure:

_____

_____

_____

_____

Scavenger Hike Adventure

Cosby Nature Trail

WHY THIS IS A GREAT TRAIL! This Scavenger Hike
Adventure is on a trail that is a hidden jewel in the
Smokies! You will enjoy the "surround sounds" of
water as you cross streams eight times on log bridges!
This trail has many huge hemlock trees, and it is
always damp and shaded by the lush, green forest.
On a hot day, this cool trail is the ticket! You'll
search for a tree that was ripped apart by a bear, a
family's garden from long ago, a tree that looks like
an elbow, and a trunk of a tree you can stand in! This
trail is on the "quiet" side of the park near Cosby, and
it is worth every single minute of the drive over! There is also
a picnic area near the trailhead. You might want to pack some
PB&Js!

WHERE'S THE TRAIL? From the Sugarlands Visitor Center, go north on U.S. Highway 441 into Gatlinburg. Veer right onto U.S. Highway 321 right past the Hard Rock Cafe at **Stoplight #3.** (Stoplights in Gatlinburg are all numbered with big signs.) Follow US 321 until you can't go any farther. At that T in the road, turn right (south) toward Cosby Campground; in about 1 mile you'll see the Cosby park entrance on the right. Drive *past* the picnic area and campground reservation office and you'll see the sign for the Cosby Nature Trail. There is a small parking area near the amphitheater.

ABOUT THE TRAIL: This EASY hike is a level walk with a nicely cleared trail of gravel, stones, and forest mulch. There are many great places to sit by the water and cool off. This dense, lush trail reminds us of the forest scene in the movie *The Wizard of Oz.* This is one of our favorite nature trails in the entire park! Don't miss it!

HOW LONG IS THIS HIKE? This Scavenger Hike Adventure is less than a mile round-trip and will take an hour or less to complete.

A BRIEF COMMENT ABOUT THE COSBY SIDE OF THE PARK: This part of the Great Smoky Mountains National Park gets minimal use because it is not close to go-cart tracks or fudge shops. It is quiet, has practically no traffic, and is an easy and scenic country drive to get there! It is a beautiful part of the park, with trails that lead to vista views and a waterfall!

THINGS TO HUNT FOR

(Earn 10 points for each treasure you find.)

1

FIND THE HOMESITE of a Family Who Lived Here Long, Long Ago!

(Left of the parking lot and just left
of the nature trailhead sign)

SPECIAL HINT: Before you enter the trail, look for the stack of rocks that was once a fireplace! Families lived throughout this area even back in the 1800s. There once was a huge apple orchard nearby! **Fireplace and chimney remains** (such as this one) or even yellow daffodils often mark the spot of a former homesite.

10 POINTS

2

FIND THE OLD WAGON ROAD!

(After you go down the little hill and get on the trail)

SPECIAL HINT: Look down the trail to your right and then to your left! Where you are now standing used to be the wagon road for the community that existed here. Amazing, isn't it? The road ran right by the old homesite you just discovered!

10 POINTS

3

FIND THE MOUNTAIN SPRING!

(As soon as you get on the trail, look down the
side of the hill toward the stream.)

SPECIAL HINT: Look for a white pipe sticking out of the side
of the hill! The water from this spring was called "free stone
water" by the local mountain people because it had few minerals in it. In other words, the water tasted sweet compared to
some spring water that contained a lot of iron or other not-so-
tasty minerals. ***Never drink any water from the
park's streams or springs without treating it by
boiling or purifying it with chemicals.*** **10 POINTS**

4

SMELL A HEMLOCK!

(On the left side of the trail—find an evergreen tree with short,
flat needles about as long as your fingernail.)

SPECIAL HINT: Check on the underside of a branch. If each
needle has two white stripes—you've found a hemlock! Gently
rub the needles of the tree between your thumb and fingers,
and then take a whiff. The next time someone asks
if you have ever really smelled a hemlock tree, say, **"Uh"** (Cherokee for
"yes") and then say, **"Zee-yookt
guh-noh-hee-ahay"** (Cherokee
for "I speak the truth"). Indians

lived in these parts for thousands of years. Many Cherokee Indians still live on the Qualla Indian Reservation on the other side of this mountain range in Cherokee, North Carolina!

10 POINTS

5

FIND THE TREE with an "Elbow"!

(On the right of the trail as you pass the amphitheater above you)

SPECIAL HINT: This tree is located *before* you get to the first stream crossing. It is very unusual because the trunk has grown in a curve that looks like a giant arm and elbow!

10 POINTS

6

FIND THE "HORNED" TREE!

(On the left side of the trail at the first stream crossing)

SPECIAL HINT: Stand at the edge of the shallow stream and look to your left. In shaded forests, such as this one, hemlock trees put all their energy "to grow" at the top, searching for the sun. That is why lower branches rot away to become these dead branches that look like "horns." The branches at the top of this tree have found the sun, and they are doing great!

10 POINTS

7

FIND THE WILD GRAPEVINE!

(Stand on the log footbridge—look to the left.)

SPECIAL HINT: Look up! This long, woody wild grapevine is growing very high in a tree! Opossums and skunks and many other Smoky Mountain critters snack on the wild grapes!

10 POINTS

8

FIND THE TREE That Was Clawed by a Black Bear!

(Go to the next footbridge—count 50 steps past the bridge, then search on the right side of the trail.)

SPECIAL HINT: Bears will often tear into trees searching for honey, grubs, termites, and other small squiggly snacks. What are you having for lunch? There are about 1,500 bears in the park, and that means there are about two bears for every square mile. Bears are often high up in the treetops. They are great climbers! Quick! Look up!

10 POINTS

9

FIND THE DOG-HOBBLE!

(At Marker #3)

SPECIAL HINT: Look for a low bush with sharp-edged leaves. Do the test, and gently rub your finger back and forth across the edges to see if they are sharp. Long ago, settlers' dogs would chase after bears and would get stuck in these bushes. They sure could make a dog "hobble." The bears would run right through. So now you know why it is called dog-hobble! While you are at this spot, check out the "eagle claw" at the top of a tree!

10 POINTS

10

FIND THE "SPIDER" TREE!

(Near Marker #4)

SPECIAL HINT: New trees will sometimes grow out of a dead tree trunk. The roots of the new tree will grow around the trunk of the *dead* tree. Years later, the dead trunk rots away and leaves roots that are standing up off the ground and sort of look like **legs of a spider!**

10 POINTS

11

FIND THE "WIZARD OF OZ" JUNGLE!

(After the next two log footbridges—as you head up a slope)

SPECIAL HINT: Trust me! As you hike up the slope, you'll *know* when you make it to the jungle, but don't expect to find a yellow brick road! The leaves of rhododendron are about as long as from the top of your head to your chin and are thick and leathery. You are in a jungle of them. Cherokee Indians, who lived here, carved pipes and toys using wood from this bush. They also placed a leaf on the forehead to cure a headache! ***Remember: Never pick or take anything from this national park! Protect every treasure you see!***   **10 POINTS**

12

FIND THE FALLEN TREE
That "Belongs" to the Stump!

(At Marker #6)

SPECIAL HINT: There is a stump on the left of the path. Search for the tree that originally was connected to that stump! The stump and the fallen tree have both become homes for moss, ferns, and other plants. They are also home for insects and possibly other Smoky Mountain critics.   **10 POINTS**

13

FIND THE SPICEBUSHES the Mountain Folks Used to Make Tea!

(On the right side of the trail at Marker #8)

SPECIAL HINT: A large stack of stones marks the location of a fireplace and the site where someone lived long, long ago. Spicebushes are all around the fireplace. They are about as tall or a little taller than a person and have thin branches. Gently rub one of the branches with your fingernail and take a whiff! Mountain folks would break up the twigs of these bushes, boil them in water, and brew up some **spicy, lemony tea!** It was also excellent seasoning for a delicious groundhog or opossum entree. Now—stay put at Marker #8. ***Remember . . . all plants are protected. Never pick or take anything from the park.***

◯

10 POINTS

14

FIND THE LOCATION OF A FAMILY GARDEN from Long, Long Ago!

(Near Marker #8—on the left side of the trail)

SPECIAL HINT: Stone walls were built one heavy stone at a time! It was hard work building these walls! Often stones had to be cleared off the land to plant a garden because the Smoky Mountains is a *very* rocky place. Three walls still encircle what was once a family's vegetable garden. On the right side of the trail is their home-

site. Speak a little Cherokee just for fun! Ask one of your fellow hikers, **"Zah-we-shah-ohsh?"** That's Cherokee for "Do you have a garden?" Your fellow hiker can answer, **"Uh,"** which means "yes," or **"Hah-dee-yoh-gah,"** which means "no."

○

10 POINTS

15

FIND THE CORNER OF ANOTHER OLD ROCK WALL!

(50 steps past Marker #8)

SPECIAL HINT: This 90-degree rock wall corner is a good place to peer into the woods and imagine where the old pasture or field once was! You are standing in the middle of what was once farm fields and pastures! Young trees are now growing back. Imagine kids playing, gardens growing, and cows mooing! Okay, time to *"moooove"* on down the trail!

○

10 POINTS

16

FIND THE MOUNTAIN FAMILY'S SOURCE OF DRINKING WATER!

(At Marker #9)

SPECIAL HINT: This mountain spring once had a small shed built around it (they called it a **springhouse**). Settlers would store milk, eggs, and some meats around the flowing water. This was their refrigerator and their drinking fountain! Notice the rocks that the mountain folks put in this hole to keep the spring opened up. Pretty cool!

○

10 POINTS

17

FIND THE "APARTMENT HOUSE TREE"
and the Grapevines Gone Wild!

(Just past Marker #10—on the left of the trail)

SPECIAL HINT: The bottom of this tree trunk looks as if it has small compartments, or maybe "apartments"! Trees provide homes for many creatures in the forest. Smoky Mountain critters may find a place to sleep in these holes. Look around! Find the huge woody **grapevines** that have gone absolutely wild! Tarzan would really like this spot!

10 POINTS

18

FIND A VIRGINIA CREEPER Creeping up a Tree!

(22 steps past Marker #10—search on the left.)

SPECIAL HINT: It looks sort of like a furry poison ivy vine but has gnarly, wormlike tentacles growing around its outside. Another clue is that it has five-leaf groupings, unlike poison ivy, which has "leaves of three." This creeper is nonpoisonous.

10 POINTS

19

FIND A TREE Growing Out of a Humongous *Stump* of Another Tree!

(On the right—after a backward S curve in the trail
—look about 15 feet into the woods.)

SPECIAL HINT: Dead tree trunks often are a very nourishing spot for a new tree to grow. Moisture, like you find on this trail, helps to make the environment perfect for dead logs to become new homes for other plants. Sometimes such a dead tree trunk is called a **nurse tree** because it is feeding and nourishing new plants and trees!

10 POINTS

20

STAND INSIDE THE TRUNK of a Tree!

(On the left—just before you reach the log footbridge)

SPECIAL HINT: *Always check for Smoky Mountain critters before entering a tree trunk!* Bears will often take a nap inside the hollow of a tree; therefore, to get the points, it is recommended that you only *stand* inside the tree trunk. Do not take a nap in there!

10 POINTS

CONGRATULATIONS!

You have just completed a

Great Smoky Mountains National Park

Scavenger Hike Adventure!

Cosby Nature Trail

10 points for each item found

Total Score _____

Certified Achievement Level _____

50 to 100 points: *City Slicker*

Over **100 to 170** points: *Pioneer Scout*

Over **170** points: *Frontier Explorer*

Name(s): _____

_____

Witness(es) thereof: _____

Date: _____

Journal Notes

The people on this hike were:

_____

_____

_____

The weather was:

_____

_____

_____

We saw:

_____

_____

_____

_____

More about our adventure:

_____

_____

_____

_____

Scavenger Hike Adventure

 and

Alum Cave Bluffs Trail and
Up to Mount LeConte

WHY THIS IS A GREAT TRAIL! Alum Cave Bluffs Trail is a humdinger of a hike! Many hikers rave that it is the most scenic hike in the Great Smoky Mountains National Park! On this Scavenger Hike Adventure you will follow **Alum Cave Creek** as you hike across many footbridges! Find *giant* hemlock trees that are hundreds of years old! Find signs of the tremendous flash flood that hit Mount LeConte on Labor Day weekend in 1951! Hike *through* the inside of a giant rock formation called **Arch Rock!** You'll find cable "handrails" to assist you in steep areas with sheer drop-offs and unbelievably incredible views! Find the needle hole in the side of a mountain, and be inspired at **Inspiration Point!** You'll find **Alum Cave Bluffs!** Whoa! It's unlike anything else you will ever see in the Great Smoky Mountains!

You may choose the ***Extremely Extreme*** option and continue on from the bluffs another strenuous 2.8 miles to Mount LeConte (elevation 6,593 feet). Mount LeConte is more than *a mile high* from its base! Along the way to Mount LeConte you will find views that will definitely—and we mean *definitely*—knock your hiking socks off! You will find the most popular rustic lodge in the east that can only be reached on foot! Sit a spell in a rocking chair! You deserve it! Check out the panoramic views from **Cliff Top!**

WHERE'S THE TRAIL? From Sugarlands Visitor Center follow the signs toward Cherokee and Newfound Gap on U.S. Highway 441 (Newfound Gap Road). At about 8.6 miles you will see a sign for Alum Cave Bluffs Trail. The trailhead and parking are on the left.

ABOUT THE TRAIL: I'm not bluffin'! You may be huffin'! All the way to Arch Rock (1.3 miles), the trail is wide and fairly level. The trail then becomes much steeper as you continue on to Alum Cave Bluffs (about 2.2 miles from the trailhead). The cable handrail helps! At times the trail is rocky and narrow.

While EXTREME this is absolutely—no doubt about it—worth tackling! Going on to Mount LeConte is strenuous and steep, but it is the most traveled route to the tippety top! **Key tip:** Allow *plenty* of time, and *take* your time.

HOW LONG IS THIS HIKE? This Scavenger Hike Adventure to Alum Cave Bluffs is 4.4 miles round-trip; allow 3 to 4 hours.

Going on up to Mount LeConte and searching around the top is about a 10.5-mile round-trip, and you should allow 6 to 8 hours or more. If you plan to hike 13 and 14 together, count on a full day! Definitely take plenty of water and plenty of food to keep up your energy on this **Extremely Extreme** Scavenger Hike Adventure! You can get more drinking water at the top for your trek down.

THINGS TO HUNT FOR

(Earn 10 points for each treasure you find.)

1

FIND HOW LONG A TROUT MUST BE to Have over to Your House for Dinner!

(Look for the sign at the trailhead.)

SPECIAL HINT: There are more than 2,000 miles of streams in the Great Smoky Mountains! That's a lot of water and a lot of fish! Some streams in the Smokies have 2,000 to 4,000 trout per mile! If you catch a trout and take it home for dinner, it better be at least ___ inches long! The national park protects the fish in these

10 POINTS

waters. As long as you follow the rules in the park, you can grab a pole and "Go fish!"

2
FIND THE OUTDOOR THERMOMETERS!
(After you cross the footbridge,
look on both sides of the trail.)

SPECIAL HINT: Do you notice any bushes with long, narrow, and thick dark-green leaves? Look really hard . . . Not! You are totally surrounded! These rhododendron leaves stay green all year and will bloom with beautiful flowers in late spring and summer! The leaves will tell you the temperature! At 32 degrees they begin to darken and droop, at 20 degrees they roll up, and at 0 degrees they roll up as tight as a pencil! How cool is that! Pioneers actually used these plants as thermometers!

10 POINTS

3
FIND THE HUMONGOUS OLD HEMLOCK TREE!
(Count 60 steps from the second footbridge—
look *across* Alum Cave Creek.)

SPECIAL HINT: Stand on a rock for the best view! This trail is home to some of the biggest and oldest trees in the park! Some hemlocks in the Smokies are 300 to 400 years old! This is an old-growth northern hardwood and hemlock forest. This area of the park has never been logged, so it looks much like it did in the days of pioneers and Indians! That's why it's called an **old-growth forest.** The beautiful hemlock trees in our park are being threatened by a tiny insect from Asia called the hemlock woolly adelgid (*a-DELL-jid*). Our park rangers are doing everything they can to save these trees!

10 POINTS

4

FIND THE GIANT "HOLEY" HEMLOCK!

(On the right—it is practically on the trail.)

SPECIAL HINT: Take a peck—I mean a peek! Woodpeckers have had a field day on this tree, pecking holes as they looked for insects! You'll find a smaller holey hemlock before you reach this giant. Trust us! You'll know when you arrive at this tree! This tree is about 20 hiking boots (lady's size 8) around! Three people arm to arm might still not make it around the trunk! The tree has thick reddish-brown bark and lacy-looking branches of needles. This trail is famous for its giant hemlock trees and yellow birches!

10 POINTS

5

FIND THE BEAR HOBBLE . . . NOT!

(40 steps past the holey tree—look on both sides of the trail.)

SPECIAL HINT: This evergreen plant *would not* hobble a bear! Pioneer dogs, though, would get stuck, or "hobbled," in these bushes as they tried to run through them to chase bears! The bears could run right through the bushes. That is why it is not called "bear hobble!" Feel the sharp edges of the leaves to make sure you've found it! Oh, by the way, it is called **dog-hobble!**

○

10 POINTS

6

FIND THE GIANT TREE ROOTS
Traveling across the Trail Searching for Food!
(Count 50 steps past the small round log that crosses the trail.)

SPECIAL HINT: *Roots are as slippery as rocks when wet! Be careful!* These tree roots are searching everywhere for food and water to keep the tree alive. The ground is very rocky in the Smoky Mountains, and the roots are doing all they can to feed the tree!

○

10 POINTS

7

FIND THE TREE Wrapped around a Boulder!
(20 steps past the huge hemlock tree on the left of the trail—in a wide-open area by the creek)

SPECIAL HINT: The tree wrapped around the boulder is on the right of the trail, and you'll see what looks like a **small cave-**

PROTECT THE GREAT SMOKY MOUNTAINS NATIONAL PARK

like opening under the rock. This yellow birch tree grew right around the rock. Very interesting! There are lots of fascinating natural sights like this in the forests of the Smokies!

10 POINTS

8

FIND A SIGN OF A BLACK BEAR!

(Anywhere along the trail—go on to #9 while you are searching.)

SPECIAL HINT: This trail is known for a lot of bear activity! Bear droppings (scat) are often a shiny blue-black in color in the berry-eating season. Another sign of bears is claw marks on trees or torn apart logs where bears searched for insects to eat. Also look for bear prints in muddy areas. Find any sign of a bear along this trail to earn the points! By the way, there are about 1,500 black bears in the national park. That means that there are about two bears for every square mile. Now, how long is this trail? All black bears in the Smokies are actually black! Black bears in other parts of our country range in color from off-white to cinnamon to chocolate brown and finally to black!

10 POINTS

9

FIND THE WALL OF ROOTS!

(Right side of the trail)

SPECIAL HINT: A tree was blown over and created a huge

"wall of roots." The forest is changing constantly. Wind, rain, snow, hail, lightning, landslides, floods, insects, and temperature changes all affect the environment. This tree faced a very heavy wind—and lost the battle. It will now serve a new purpose as a home for many animals and plants!

10 POINTS

10

FIND THE TWO YELLOW BIRCH TREES!

(30 steps past the wall of roots—search on the right for two birch trees standing side by side.)

SPECIAL HINT: The bark is yellowish or silvery-white in color. The yellow birch tree bark is shaggy in spots and looks like shreds of paper. The bark has horizontal lines, not vertical like most other trees. This tree was very important to Indians and pioneers because its bark has oil in it and burns even when it is wet. Since birch wood burns slowly and gives off lots of heat, mountain folks would use it for baking bread and pies.

10 POINTS

11

FIND THE WHITE QUARTZ ROCKS!

(Breathe deep; it will take a while to get there. Look for the leaning tree that is smack-dab in the middle of the trail—look up the hill on the left to find the rocks.)

SPECIAL HINT: Quartz is the most common of all minerals and is found throughout the Smokies. There is another really cool quirk of nature at this stop. Turn around and find the rock that is lodged in a tree at *eye level* on the opposite side of the trail! Nature is amazing!!! **10 POINTS**

12

FIND THE NURSING TREE TRUNK!

(Count back 45 steps from the leaning tree and quartz rocks of #11 toward *the start* of the trail—look up the hill to the right as you face the trailhead.)

SPECIAL HINT: Find the huge rhododendron shrub that is growing right out of the top of a tall dead tree trunk. The tree trunk is like a "mother" nursing the plant with food and nutrients. This occurs because there is so much rain and moisture in these woods. At this elevation more than 80 inches (almost 7 feet) of rain falls each year. You'll see many plants and bushes growing out of stumps and even out of dead trees high off the ground. **10 POINTS**

13
FIND THE SLATE HIGHWAY!
(Just before you reach the log footbridge)

SPECIAL HINT: This rock pathway can be slippery when wet. It is made of slate and **Anakeesta rock.** Why do we call it a *high-way*? It's a *way* to get to *higher* places along this trail! Up ahead . . . Alum Cave Bluffs! Mount LeConte!

○

10 POINTS

14
FIND THE YELLOW BIRCH HANDRAIL!
(At the next log footbridge)

SPECIAL HINT: Think . . . shaggy paperlike bark; yellowish tint; shiny horizontal lines; used for baking pies . . . ringing any bells?

○

10 POINTS

15
CONDUCT A SCIENTIFIC EXPERIMENT!
(20 steps past the log footbridge)

SPECIAL HINT: Find the half dozen or so evergreen trees on the left side of the trail. Touch the end of a tree needle; if it hurts, you have identified a red spruce tree! If it feels soft and you didn't say "Ouch," it is a hemlock! OK. You're now a forestry scientist . . . Not! To be extra sure it is a hemlock, check for two white stripes on the underside of each needle.

○

10 POINTS

16

FIND THE JUMBLED UP TREES, Rocks, Stumps, and Bushes Left Here by the 1951 Labor Day Weekend Flash Flood on Mount LeConte!

(As you bear to the right—up the hill)

SPECIAL HINT: On Labor Day Weekend in 1951, a powerful storm dumped a huge amount of rain *in just 1 hour in one small area on Mount LeConte!* The flash flood came hurling down the mountain carrying large trees, boulders, shrubs, rocks, and dirt toward the bottom of the mountain. The debris is still here. Find it and earn the points. Farther up the trail is debris from another major storm that occurred in 1993 when a 20-foot avalanche of water crashed down from Mount LeConte! Do you have your poncho with you? **10 POINTS**

17

FIND A BLACK-BELLIED SALAMANDER!

(Look under rocks and branches along the creek and along wet mossy banks and in damp areas of the trail.)

SPECIAL HINT: There are 31 different kinds of salamanders in the park. They are camouflaged and very hard to see. Look

very very closely after you pick up a rock. If you find one, don't put the rock back on top of the salamander because you might hurt it. Go ahead and give yourself the points for any salamander that you see! The **black-bellied salamander** is more than 6 inches long and is probably the largest of the salamanders living on this trail. It has a black belly and often has a double row of light dots on its sides. The **hellbender salamander** grows to more than 2 feet long! Whoa! The damp area around Arch Rock is a great place to look.

10 POINTS

18

FIND THE ARCH ROCK AND BENCH!

(You can't miss either of these treasures—straight ahead.)

SPECIAL HINT: You'll be happy to find both of these treasures! The arch is made of **Anakeesta rock,** which is actually oceanic mud (mud from the ocean) that was squished together really . . . I mean *really* hard. Scientists believe that rock was turned to mud when the continents collided millions of years ago and produced intense pressure and heat. **Anakeesta** is a Cherokee word meaning "Place of the Balsams," referring to the Fraser fir trees that grow farther up the mountain. It is hard to believe that where you are walking was once the BOTTOM of an ocean! You will now *walk right through the center of this rock formation!* There are steel cables to help you.

10 POINTS

19

FIND INSPIRATION POINT!

(Hike quite a while—located at the top of a ridge
where the trail takes a 90-degree turn to the right)

SPECIAL HINT: The lookout over this rock cliff offers an
incredible view of the valleys and hills far below! Are you
inspired yet? ***Be careful.*** You are standing on a rock at more
than 4,500 feet elevation with a long, sheer drop to the bottom!
A little red squirrel called the **"mountain boomer"** is often seen
along this trail with the little gray junco bird called the **"snow-
bird."** Inspiration Point is on a **heath bald,** which is an area
with lots of low-growth plants like catawba rhododendron,
mountain laurel, and sand myrtle *instead* of trees. The catawba
rhododendron near Inspiration Point has beauti-
ful purple and pink flowers that bloom in late
spring and early summer! **10 POINTS**

20

FIND THE NEEDLE HOLE IN THE MOUNTAIN!

(Stop and look to your left as you get to
the steel-cable handrail.)

SPECIAL HINT: Look in the distance and find
the round hole that goes *all the way* through the
top of **Little Duck Hawk Ridge!** Look along the
horizon at the top of the mountains to find the
hole. A "duck hawk" is what the mountain folks

called the peregrine falcon. Peregrines can dive out of the sky at speeds of more than 180 miles per hour to grab prey (other birds) in midair! Talk about fast food! Peregrine falcons were reintroduced to the park in the 1980s and can again be found along this trail. **10 POINTS**

21

FIND THE ROCK OVERHANG
That Is About as Big as a Football Field!
(Alum Cave Bluffs are so awesome they
will take your breath away.)

SPECIAL HINT: Believe me—you won't find anything else like the bluffs in these Smoky Mountains! You are standing about 5,000 feet above sea level and are about halfway to Mount LeConte! These cliffs are **Anakeesta rock** just like the **Arch Rock** you went through earlier in the hike. The bluffs are not really a cave, and there never really was any alum up here! This is a massive rock overhang that was once mined for epsom salts! The sulfur in the bluffs smells a bit like rotten eggs. *Be wary of falling icicles in the winter!* **10 POINTS**

CONGRATULATIONS!

You have just completed a

Great Smoky Mountains National Park

Scavenger Hike Adventure!

Alum Cave Bluffs Trail to the Bluffs

10 points for each item found

Total Score _____

Certified Achievement Level _____

50 to 100 points: *City Slicker*

Over **100 to 180** points: *Pioneer Scout*

Over **180** points: *Frontier Explorer*

Name(s): _____

_____

Witness(es) thereof: _____

Date: _____

Journal Notes

The people on this hike were:

_____

_____

_____

The weather was:

_____

_____

_____

We saw:

_____

_____

_____

More about our adventure:

_____

_____

_____

_____

_____

Scavenger Hike Adventure

Extremely Extreme Option to Hike 13

on Up to Mount LeConte

22
FIND "GRACIE'S PULPIT"!
(10- to 15-minute hike past the bluffs—search on the left.)

SPECIAL HINT: This is a rocky lookout point named for **Gracie McNichol,** who climbed Mount LeConte more than 200 times, including on her 92nd birthday! How old are you?

10 POINTS

Put your book away and enjoy the incredible 2.5 miles on up to the top of Mount LeConte!!! Your next search item is 2.5 miles from where you are standing right now!

23

FIND THE NAME OF THE MAN Who Carried His Mother to Mount LeConte While She Was Strapped to his Back Sitting in a Kitchen Chair!

(Search in the "Office.")

SPECIAL HINT: This is no joke! Find the photo-graph on the wall.

10 POINTS

24

FIND THE SNAGS!

(On the mountain slopes)

SPECIAL HINT: Fraser fir and red spruce trees grow up high here on Mount LeConte. The thousands of dead Fraser fir trees (called "snags") surrounding you were infested by the tiny bal-sam woolly adelgid (*a-DELL-jid*) insect that came from Europe. It killed 95 percent of the mature trees in the park. You can see how very beautiful these Fraser fir trees were because you can

find some of the younger generation of trees up on this mountain. Forest rangers hope that some of the young seedlings from a few mature trees that survived the attack up here on Mount LeConte have inherited a resistance to the bug. They are hopeful that this new generation of trees will reforest this area of the park.

10 POINTS

25
FIND THE STREET SIGN
That Says Llama Lane!
(Behind the kitchen)

SPECIAL HINT: Llamas bring food and clean sheets and pillowcases up to the lodge at Mount LeConte. They trek up on **Trillium Gap Trail,** one of the five trails that reach this summit. Llamas have smaller and softer hooves than horses, and they cause less damage to the trails.

10 POINTS

26
FIND CLIFF TOP!
(As unbelievable as it may sound—hike up!
Follow the sign to Cliff Top!)

SPECIAL HINT: Cliff Top or bust! It is only ²⁄₁₀ of a mile from the rustic cabins and lodges of Mount LeConte. The view is absolutely magnificent on a clear day! There is a huge flat rock area at Cliff Top that is suitable for taking an extremely well-deserved break. Enjoy your journey back down. Remember, the journey *is* the destination!

10 POINTS

CONGRATULATIONS!

You have just completed a

Great Smoky Mountains National Park

Scavenger Hike Adventure!

Alum Cave Bluffs Trail to the Bluffs and Extremely Extreme Option on Up to Mount LeConte

10 points for each item found

Total Score _____

Certified Achievement Level _____

50 to 100 points: *City Slicker*

Over **100 to 210** points: *Pioneer Scout*

Over **210** points: *Frontier Explorer*

Name(s): _____

_____

Witness(es) thereof: _____

Date: _____

Journal Notes

The people on this hike were:

_____

_____

_____

The weather was:

_____

_____

_____

We saw:

_____

_____

_____

_____

More about our adventure:

_____

_____

_____

_____

Keep Exploring the Smokies!

Here Are Some Great Books!

We listened to a lot of park rangers, mountain folks, park resident descendants, and other locals to research the hidden treasures. We also studied some great books, listed below. Most of them are available in the Great Smoky Mountains National Park visitor centers or at the Great Smoky Mountains Association's online bookstore at www.SmokiesStore.org.

Alsop, Fred J. III. *Birds of the Smokies* (Great Smoky Mountains Association, 2001).

Boyd, Brian A. *Great Smoky Mountains Pocket Companion* (Fern Creek Press, 2001).

Brewer, Carson. *Day Hikes of the Smokies* (Great Smoky Mountains Association, 2002).

———. *Hiking in the Great Smokies* (Newman/National, 1962).

Brown, Gary. *Outwitting Bears, Living in Bear Country* (Lyons Press, 2001).

Delaughter, Jerry. *Mountain Roads & Quiet Places* (Great Smoky Mountains Association, 1986).

Duncan, Barbara R., and Brett H. Riggs. *Cherokee Heritage Trails Guidebook* (in association with the Museum of the Cherokee Indian and University of North Carolina Press, 2003).

Dunn, Durwood. *Cades Cove, The Life and Death of a Southern Appalachian Community, 1818–1837* (University of Tennessee Press, 1988).

Frome, Michael. *Strangers in High Places, The Story of the Great Smoky Mountains* (University of Tennessee Press, 1997).

Gilmore, Robert. *Great Walks, The Great Smokies* (Great Walks, Inc., 1992).

Great Smoky Mountains Association. *Hiking Trails of the Smokies,* 3rd ed. (2003).

Grooms, Don, and John Oocumma. *How to Talk Trash in Cherokee* (Downhome Publishing, 1989).

Hollowell, Anne C. and Barbara G. *Fern Finder* (Nature Study Guild).

Houk, Rose. *Great Smoky Mountains National Park, A Natural History Guide* (Houghton Mifflin, 1993).

Hubbs, Hal, Charles Maynard, and David Morris. *Time Well Spent, Family Hiking in the Smokies,* 3rd ed. (Panther Press, 1995).

Jenkins, Ken (photographer), and Carson Brewer. *Great Smoky Mountains National Park* (Graphic Arts Center Publishing).

Malloy, Johnny. *Day and Overnight Hikes in the Great Smoky Mountains National Park,* 2nd ed. (Menasha Ridge Press, 2001).

Mooney, James. *History, Myths and Sacred Formulas of the Cherokees* (originally published by the Bureau of American Ethnology, 1891; Bright Mountain Books, 1992).

Oakley, Harvey and Melba. *Smoky Mountains Memories and Meditations* (Oakley Books, 2003).

Oakley, Wiley. *Roamin' & Restin'* (Oakley Books, 1940).

Ogle, Lucinda Oakley. *Remembrances of My Past 93 Years Growing Up in the Great Smoky Mountains* (published by L. O. Oakley, 2002).

Roop, Peter and Connie. *If You Lived with the Cherokee* (Scholastic, Inc., 1998).

Russell, Gladys Trentham. *Smoky Mountain Family Album* (published by Russell Publishing Company, 1984).

———. *It Happened in the Smokies* (published by Russell Publishing Company, 1988).

Schneider, Bill and Russ. *Backpacking Tips* (The Globe Pequot Press, 2005).

Shields, Randolph A. *The Cades Cove Story* (Great Smoky Mountains Association, 1981).

Tilley, Stephen G., and James E. Huheey. *Reptiles and Amphibians of the Great Smoky Mountains* (Great Smoky Mountains Association, 2001).

Weals, Vic. *Legends of Cades Cove and the Smokies Beyond* (Olden Press, 2002).

White, Peter (lead author). *Wildflowers of the Smokies* (Great Smoky Mountains Association, 1996).

Wise, Kenneth, *Hiking Trails of the Great Smoky Mountains* (University of Tennessee Press, 1996).

Wise, Kenneth, and Ron Petersen. *A Natural History of Mount LeConte* (University of Tennessee Press, 1998).

Wuerthner, George. *Great Smoky Mountains, A Visitors Companion* (Stackpole Books, 2003).

Two Cherished Friends in the Smokies

‘

ILLUSTRATOR G WEBB

It is a special gift to have G Webb as our friend, and it is a treasure to have him join us in our Scavenger Hike Adventures
interactive hiking series as artistic guide and illustrator. G
Webb teaches Sunday School at our little church by the creek,
has created a beautiful vineyard (that looks more like a paint-
ing than a farm), and is an active leader and benefactor in our
little mountain community of Pittman Center, Tennessee.
Somehow he has also found time to become a nationally
renowned watercolor artist.

When you visit the Smokies, please stop on by his 1910 restored
homestead gallery in the Great Smoky Mountains Arts and Crafts

Community and linger for a
while. You'll be visiting a
cherished friend of the
Smokies and of ours;
www.Gwebbgallery.com.

GREAT SMOKY MOUNTAINS ASSOCIATION

The Great Smoky Mountains National Park has no admission fee and 20 percent of its operating budget comes from volunteerism and donations. It is truly the "people's park." Our friends at the Great Smoky Mountains Association (GSMA) manage all the official national park visitor centers' stores and help raise funds to support this incredible world-famous wonder. They were authorized by Congress to support the park's educational, scientific, and historical programs. The GSMA has supported the concept of our interactive hiking guide from the original idea to its achievement of regional best-seller status. Please stop by any of the national park's visitor centers and get to know another cherished friend of the Smokies, the Great Smoky Mountains Association; www.smokiesstore.org.

DATE			